LISTEN...
IT WILL CHANGE YOUR LIFE

A Practical Guide to Effective Listening and Communication

Charles Page

PARK PLACE PUBLICATIONS
PACIFIC GROVE, CALIFORNIA

Listen – It Will Change Your Life!
A Practical Guide to Effective Listening and Communication

by Charles Page
Edited by Joelle Steele
Copyright 2002

All rights reserved under International and Pan-American copyright conventions. No part of this book may be used or reproduced in any manner whatsoever without written permission except in the case of brief quotations embodied in critical articles or reviews. For information, address Park Place Publications, P.O. Box 829, Pacific Grove, CA 93950.

ISBN 1-877809-96-9
Library of Congress Control Number: 2002115082
Printed in United States of America
First U.S. Edition: 2002

On-line at www.parkplace-publications.com

Dedication

I dedicate this book to my late wife, Caroline. A marriage of 50 years requires that both parties learn to listen effectively. We worked at it, including counseling that enabled both of us to become better listeners. Listening effectively is the most difficult during the inevitable stresses and strains of life that we all experience. But these are the very moments when listening effectively is most vital. Caroline was diagnosed with a vicious cancer, Multiple Myeloma, in 1996. She was informed that she had no more than two and one-half years to live. She fought courageously and lived for five years. Notwithstanding severe pain and intrusive chemotherapy, she lived life to the fullest until three weeks before her death; she continued her work in various community projects, traveled, nourished her family and friends, and brought joy to a remarkable variety of people throughout the world. During her cancer journey we both learned a lot about the importance of effective listening.

Acknowledgments

So many people have shared their knowledge with me and inspired me to write this book. I thank my late wife, Caroline, who encouraged me and put up with me during my efforts; my many inspired and inspiring teachers; Lewis Fenton, my mentor and law partner; Charles Keller, a law partner from whom I learned a lot about effective listening; my wonderful sons, Stephen, David, Christopher, and Jeff; my daughters-in-law, Judy, Heather, and Farnoosh, who listened to me; my grandchildren who are very good listeners; and my many friends and colleagues with whom I have worked while trying to make our community a better place, and from whom I learned many of the lessons set forth herein.

If this book is easy to read and flows in an effective way I am forever grateful to my editor Joelle Steele who was patient, helpful, and encouraging. Ernest Hemingway reportedly said: "You never finish a book, you abandon it." Joelle helped me <u>finish</u> this book.

CONTENTS

Preface vii

Introduction x

Chapter 1: Master These Listening Techniques 1
  The Need To Listen; Decide – I'm Going To Listen; Get Ready – Now Listen; Step One: You Must Relax and Focus (R&F); Step Two: Spot These Listening Barriers; Step Three: Hurdle Those Listening Barriers; Step Four: Did I Really Understand?; Write It Down; Hearing Impairment As A Listening Barrier

Chapter 2: Practice, Practice, Practice! 15
  Listen To Yourself; How Do I Persuade People To Listen To Me?

Chapter 3: Listen At Work 28
  Ask Skillful Questions; In Life's Essential Interviews – Listen

Chapter 4: Difficult Listening 40
  The Stream-of-Consciousness Monologue; Misplaced Anger; Impossible Individuals; Dealing With Emotional Overload; People Who Cannot Accept Compliments; Indecisive People – Help Them Decide; Handling Criticism; Offering Criticism and Listening To The Response

Chapter 5: Discussions And Arguments 61
  A Dose Of Reality

Chapter 6: Handling Problem Personalities 69
Problem Personalities In Groups And Meetings; Encouraging Input from The Quiet Ones; Obtaining Information Without Being Confrontational; Concluding Meetings; Listening in Public Meetings

Chapter 7: A Garden Variety Of Listening Situations .. 86
Listening Between The Lines - Separating the Message from the Words; Cross-Cultural Listening; Listening & Responding To Children; Listening to Children Who Are Not Family Members; The Dating Scene; Listening and Responding To Questions; When You Don't Have All The Answers; Communicating with Doctors, Lawyers, And Accountants; Telling a Good Joke & Anecdote; ... And In Conclusion ...

Appendices 110
A Listening Checklist; Charlie's 34 Precepts For Living a Satisfying and Fulfilling Life

Bibliography 118

About The Author 119

Preface

I am a bright, charming, witty, sparkling conversationalist. Now for a second opinion. My late wife, Caroline, would probably say, "Loquacious! He never stops talking. I have a hard time getting a word in. He never listens." In fact she might paraphrase Henny Youngman: "I haven't talked to Charlie in a week. I didn't want to interrupt him!" I'm sure that many times she has thought or said, "Charlie will do anything I say, except listen to me" or "When it appears that Charlie is listening, he is thinking about something else."

Okay, I admit it. I enjoy good conversation. Of course some might say that what I really enjoy is talking. It's all in the ear of the beholder. But listening skills have always been important in my life too.

As a student at Stanford Law School I concentrated on what teachers said, and I took prolific notes. I am blessed with – Caroline would say "cursed with" – a good memory, and I have *almost* total recall of what people say, *when* I am listening to them. But it was the *almost* and the *when* that were the problems.

When I became a practicing lawyer, I took notes when interviewing clients and discussing problems with them, but not in the same way that I did in college and law school. Then one day I was in a meeting with my clients, our opponents, their lawyer, and an arbitrator. The facts and the issues were complicated. I noticed that the arbitrator was taking notes as if he were in a law school class. After both sides had spelled out their version of the facts and issues, the arbitrator played back what he had heard. I had definitely missed some key points.

That experience was a wake-up call for me. Up until that moment, I had always been proud of my ability to hear everything that was said in meetings, to distill the essence of those conversations, and to summarize what had been said. But after this experience I realized that no one has a perfect memory. I needed to take notes so that I wouldn't miss anything.

One of my clients kept a stack of specially made cards on his desk. They had rounded corners and fit in a shirt pocket. I noticed him jotting down notes, one card for each point, writing something like "Call Harry" when he deferred a phone call during our meeting. Since I always seek out "tools" that will make my life easier and more efficient, I immediately ordered a supply of those cards. I "never leave home without them." As a result, I seldom miss important points in conversations. More importantly, when I'm involved in dynamic situations where hellzapoppin' and tensions and emotions are raging, I don't have to rely on a tricky memory.

Through my many years of practicing law, working on community projects, and serving on boards of directors, I learned other valuable listening techniques that changed my life. They enabled me to improve my relationships, achieve success as a lawyer, and be a community leader. Once I had fully assimilated these skills, their logic and usefulness seemed so obvious. I often wondered why more people did not exercise these same skills to improve their lives. Eventually, it occurred to me that the logic and usefulness of these techniques are "obvious" only after they are presented in a coherent, understandable form, with examples that demonstrate how they work and what they can achieve.

So, I inventoried and analyzed what I had learned and then organized it all into lessons that I could use in training young lawyers and in working with boards and groups that I chaired. This book is an effort to identify the barriers to effective listening, and to define workable techniques for overcoming them, both in the workplace and in your personal life. When you really learn how to listen, it will change your life.

Introduction

Yogi Berra, the master of the malaprop, gave birth to such famous observations as: "It's déjà vu all over again" and "When you come to a fork in the road, take it." He once yelled to the players in the dugout: "You can observe a lot by just watching." If Yogi were writing this book he might say "You can hear a lot by just listening!"

A television program offered a poignant piece on a special course that is required for medical residents in oncology, those doctors who will be specializing in working with and treating cancer patients. It was a course on listening. The interviewer commented to the doctor who designed the course: "This seems like common sense!" The doctor responded, "You're right. It is common sense. But when we become so focused on the medication and the various forms of treatment it is easy to forget that the most important thing is to listen to the patient."

My niece is a resident in a family practice. After reading the first draft of this book, she observed that much of what was included had been a part of her training. She commented that the book did a good job of presenting effective listening techniques, but that "it may not be a book for people with my education, training, and experience." Is this book UNnecessary for those who are trained in therapeutic listening and counseling? Not according to an article by Sandra G. Boodman in The Washington Post. Her article opens with the following:

"He doesn't listen…"
"She repeatedly interrupts you…"
"He's cold and dismissive…"

While these may sound like the typical complaints of a couple headed for divorce court, they are, in fact, the "same accusations that are frequently leveled by disgruntled patients against their doctors, often as they are about to dump their physicians and find someone new." Boodman quotes Terry Stein, an internist and director of clinician-patient communication at Kaiser Permanente Medical Group in Northern California: "The No. 1 reason patients dump their doctors is that they don't feel listened to or cared for." Boodman concludes, "Developing communication skills is regarded as something of a frill in medical education, which emphasizes more concrete skills – 'find it and fix it approach.'"

Doctors, lawyers, business executives, government executives, and executives of non-profit organizations must have effective listening skills in order to become and remain successful. They all listen in disciplined settings. Some are professionally trained to listen in therapeutic practices. Yet, I am frequently surprised at how often these same individuals fail to apply their listening techniques outside of the workplace. When they go home at the end of the day, they leave their stethoscopes and their listening skills at the office.

Perhaps this unwillingness to listen is a cultural issue. In *The Other Side of Language-A Philosophy of Listening*, author Gemma Corradi Fiumara argues that our Western Culture is antagonistic to listening, stating: "there is no such thing as a method of learning to listen to something." Fiumara further observes:

No one would deny that talking necessarily implies listening, and yet no one bothers to point out, for example, that in our culture there has always been a vast profusion of scholarly works focusing on expressive activity and very few, almost none in comparison, devoted to the study of listening.

Maybe that is at the heart of it all; the simple reason why we don't listen well is that no one ever taught us how!

Before receiving formal education children learn to speak their family language or languages. They become fluent, conceptualize and communicate ideas, deal with day to day problems with their parents, siblings, and friends, play complicated games, and create play activity. Even though they develop an amazing language facility, we know that they must have formal training in the fundamentals of their language and then practice those fundamentals. We require that they study the structure, vocabulary, and literature of their language throughout most of their schooling.

We know that our children must have effective communication skills in order to function successfully in our complex society. We know that it would be foolish to assume that formal language education is unnecessary merely because they speak and understand the language.

We do not assume that someone can watch others play golf or tennis and grab a racquet or a club and play those games. We analyze the components of the games, organize them into a course, and teach the fundamentals to anyone with a desire to play. We also know that unless a person practices those techniques s/he will never achieve competence in the activity. After making a fantastic chip shot, golfer Gary Player's ball curved across the green and into the hole. A spectator yelled out: "Lucky shot!" Player nodded, smiled, and observed: "Yep, the harder I practice the luckier I get!"

We know that good listening skills are essential for success in human relationships. But we do not offer listening courses in our schools. Why don't we teach, study, and practice listening in an organized and structured format? Why don't we teach listening the way we teach language skills? Why don't we develop and practice listening skills just like we develop and practice other skills that are essential to success in and enjoyment of life?

Is it possible that some children suspected of having Attention Deficit Disorder (ADD) have never learned how to listen? A friend who read the manuscript of this book concluded that many people have what he characterized as (LDD) Listening Deficit Disorder.

Listening is a learnable skill. It can be analyzed, broken down into essential components and organized into a useful course. But in order to develop effective listening skills and habits, as we do with our language and other desirable activities, we must acknowledge that we don't know how to listen effectively.

If we acknowledge that "listening" is a skill that is essential to living a satisfying and fulfilling life; one in which we need training and practice, we can then embark on an effort to develop effective listening skills and habits.

But, can we assume that everyone knows the importance of effective listening? My experience suggests that this is not a safe assumption. As philosopher George Santayana once observed: "Those who cannot remember the past are condemned to repeat it." Those who do not develop effective listening skills and habits may be condemned to a life of frustrations, misunderstandings, irritations, and problem relationships.

Listening requires more than just hearing what the other person is saying. It requires an attentiveness and sensitivity to the speaker. In order to be effective listeners we must develop and practice techniques that will enable us to hear what is being said in what is said.

How often do you experience the feeling that no one is listening to you? How frequently do you feel that your spouse, significant other, children, friends, fellow workers, boss, doctors, or others upon whom you depend for essential services, are not listening to you?

What do you feel when you realize that someone has not listened and has missed the point of what you are saying? How can you tell if you listen effectively?

> *Anyone who listens is fundamentally open. Without this kind of openness to one another there is no genuine human relationship; belonging together always also means being able to listen to one another.*
> – H.G. Gadamer, *Truth and Method*

Do you ever hear your spouse, significant other, your children, friends, fellow workers, or boss say: "You're not listening to me! You're missing my point!" Think about how you feel when you realize that someone is not listening to you, and then consider how your spouse, children, friends, fellow workers, or your boss feel when they think that you are not listening to them!

Consider the range of problems that adversely impact relationships when a pattern of ineffective listening occurs repeatedly:

Feelings: Frustration, irritation, stress, and "Oh, what the hell, this is never going to work!"
Results: Misunderstandings, missed opportunities, and failed projects.
Consequences: Alienation from family and friends, unhappy relationships, family breakups, job difficulties or lost jobs, failed business deals, and a myriad of other problems.

Is this an overstatement? I don't think so. Here is some anecdotal evidence that is just based on my own life and my experiences as a student, a husband, a father of four, grandfather of 6, a lawyer for 42 years, a member of boards of directors of multiple community organizations and businesses, and the Foreman of the 1996 Monterey County Civil Grand Jury.

Practically every married female to whom I mentioned that I was writing a book on effective listening remarked, "As soon as it's published, let me know. I want one for my husband!" A similar comment came from most males: "I want one for my wife!"

My friends who are business owners or managers wanted a copy for their employees. (Their employees probably wanted a copy for the owner or manager.)

I talked to many young people, students, workers, friends, and friends of my children. Their response to the idea of a book on listening was sad, but pointed and significant, "I'll buy one for my parents" (or "my teachers" or "my boss").

I talked to people in government and they wanted a copy for their staff and employees.

During my year as Grand Jury Foreman, I found that although most of the jury members were well educated, had good backgrounds and experience, and were dedicated to excellence, many lacked good listening skills. Their inability to listen effectively interfered with our task of collecting accurate information and testimony and preparing quality reports. I ended up conducting training courses in listening for the jury that proved to be effective and appreciated.

Does all this mean that ineffective listening is the sole cause of strained relationships, family alienation, family break ups, problems in the work place, in organizations, frustrations in daily efforts to arrange for and obtain essential services? No. Is ineffective listening a significant contributing cause of these problems? Yes!

Changing doctors because yours isn't listening to you may be a major disruption in your life, but it is not a traumatic life experience. But family alienation, family break-ups, and job problems are traumatic. Learning to listen is a giant step towards living a successful, satisfying, and fulfilling life.

The Importance of Listening

When I ask you to listen to me,
   And you start giving me advice,
You have not done what I asked.
When I ask that you listen to me,
And you begin to tell me why I shouldn't feel that way,
You are trampling on my feelings.
When I ask you to listen to me,
And you feel you have to do something to solve my problems,
You have failed me, strange as that may seem.
Listen: All that I ask is that you listen,
Not talk or do – just hear me.
When you do something for me
That I need to do for myself,
You contribute to my fear and feelings of inadequacy.
But when you accept as a simple fact
That I do feel what I feel, no matter how irrational,
Then I can quit trying to convince you
And go about the business
Of understanding what's behind my feelings.
So, please listen and just hear me
And, if you want to talk,
Wait a minute for your turn –
And I'll listen to you.

          – author unknown, quoted in an Ann Landers column

XVIII

Chapter 1

Master These Listening Techniques

There are no magic buttons or formulas that will enable you to instantly cure your listening problems. But there are some techniques you can learn and practice that will enable you to be a more effective listener. Remember, we are talking about a process of learning and practicing.

The Need To Listen

Life confronts us with a vast variety of listening experiences from casual, off-handed remarks to circumstances where, if we do not listen and learn, our well-being or our life might be at stake. We always need to be listening. Of course, we need to distinguish between banter at the water cooler and social chatter as we move through crowded gatherings and exchanges, no matter how brief, during which important messages are being sent. But, while different listening techniques are required for different circumstances, there are some basic components of effective listening that apply to every situation.

As the two following stories illustrate, listening at gatherings requires an alert posture and a filtering system

Mary's wedding was the social event of the season. Her cousin and bridesmaid, Jane, was from out of town and didn't know anyone.

Jane had politely greeted guests in the receiving line for an hour, when she realized that no one was listening to her. They just hurried through the line on their way to drink champagne and chat with their friends.

Jane decided to exert her irreverent sense of humor. As she greeted the guests she said, "I'm the bride's cousin, my mother just died."

"Yes, Mary was a beautiful bride," was the universal response.

"Did you hear that Warren Buffett's stock went from $600 a share to $900 a share in six months?" said a guest at a party.

"Who is Warren Buffett?" I asked.

"Only the smartest investor in the world!" said the speaker, looking at me as if I were Rip Van Winkle.

This sounded like a good opportunity to get started in investing. But I was not going to buy one share of stock for $900! I read up on Buffett, then wisely waited until the price of his stock, Berkshire Hathaway, went "down" from $900 to $2,100 a share, and bought two shares. That stock now trades for over $60,000 a share.

That little tidbit overheard at a party changed my life and my net worth!

---

that will enable you to pick up important signals and messages and filter out banter and chatter. It pays to have your antenna out and filter through the chatter even in crowded gatherings. You never know what you might hear.

Decide - I'm Going To Listen

To be a successful listener you must make a conscious decision to listen. To do so, you must first recognize a "Listening Event."

A "Listening Event" (LE) is the point in time, a fleeting moment on the run or a time that you have set aside, when you want to, need to, or have to listen and understand what is being said. The LE may be when a speaker needs to vent, get something off his or her chest, or when an issue or a problem requires discussion of alternatives and exchange of ideas. It may lead to your having to take action.

Even if the LE happens spontaneously or on the run, merely being conscious of and acknowledging to yourself that this is a "Listening Event"

is a significant step in the process of being an effective listener.
Once you recognize the LE, you must decide to listen. When the LE occurs ask yourself:

1. Do I have the time to listen right now?
2. Am I distracted by other things that demand my immediate attention?

If there is no obvious urgency, you don't have time, and are distracted, inform the other person of this and ask them if there is a better time when you can sit down with them without such distractions. If the matter just cannot wait, stop what you are doing, say to the other person, "Just a second, I need to jot something down first so that I don't forget it." They will understand that you do have other things that demand your attention. Then, take a deep breath, clear your head for a few seconds, and then focus on and listen to what is being said.

Get Ready · Now Listen

Frequently you will be confronted with situations where the speaker is fully engaged with his or her concern and will not be sensitive to what you are involved in, or what you are dealing with at that moment. In order to listen effectively the burden is on you to be sensitive to the mood of the speaker and the state of his or her awareness of your situation and the surrounding circumstances at that moment. Making the speaker aware, in a friendly way, of your desire to listen and any distractions that will interfere with your ability to listen will be mutually beneficial.

You must be aware of and alert to the status of those who are trying to communicate with you. Recognizing your comfort level and intimacy with the other person and being aware of their comfort level and feeling of intimacy with you, is important. Are you communicating with an authority figure, a boss for example, or are you the authority figure, dealing with an employee or one of your children? Or, are you on an equal footing, dealing with a spouse, a friend, or a partner?

Each of these situations will involve subtle differences in how to approach the listening event. But effective listening in each of these relationships will require that you be relaxed and focused, sincere, and yourself! (That is, being yourself *after* you have learned and practiced these listening skills!)

Step One: You Must Relax and Focus (R&F)

One of the most important books I have read is "The Relaxation Response." It had a significant influence on how I live my life, and I have since given the book to family members and friends who found it helpful. If you have agreed to listen to the other person and the time has come to do so, the Relax & Focus Mode described in "The Relaxation Response" can help prepare you for effective listening.

Relax? Focus? Seems impossible at times. After all, we are bombarded daily with TVs, radios, telephones, elevator music, noisy restaurants, traffic, sirens, aircraft, and numerous other noisy sources. And, this pervasive ambient noise level is further complicated by the many verbally expressed needs and demands of our spouses, partners, children, and grandchildren; our multiple relationships and responsibilities in the workplace; recreation and social activities; and the handling of life's logistics.

But, if you will practice this technique for a few weeks, you will find that even in the most stressful and demanding situations you can, in less than a minute, achieve a state of relaxation which will enable you to focus and enhance your listening skills.

Once you have assimilated this routine you will be able to relax and focus by taking a minute and putting yourself into an instantaneous meditative state. I try to take a moment once an hour to relax and do this. It can work wonders – even if no listening event is occurring.

> **Step One: Relax & Focus**
>
> How you use the Relax & Focus Mode depends on how much time it takes you to relax and focus, and how much time you can spare. This is a conscious and deliberate process that must be sincere both in words and body language.
>
> Find a quiet spot where you will be free from distractions and interruptions for 3 to 10 minutes. (Twenty minutes is ideal.).
>
> Sit upright in a comfortable chair. Breathe deeply and concentrate on your toes. Focus on relaxing your toes. Once you feel they are relaxed follow the same process up your calves, thighs, buttocks, arms, hands, shoulders, neck, and tongue.
>
> Once your entire body is relaxed, purge your mind. Force yourself to repeat, very slowly, in your head, not audibly, the word "one." Why "one"? For most of us the word "one" has no associations or baggage which are distracting. While reciting the word "one" over and over again, be sure that your tongue is not in action forming the words. This should purge your mind of any distracting "gotta's," "should's" and "have to's."

- Once you have relaxed and focused, join the other person in a setting that is free from distractions and interruptions.

> ### Step Two: Spot Those Listening Barriers
>
> It is difficult or impossible to listen effectively if you are on the other side of a wall from the speaker. But we erect walls; barriers that interfere with our ability to listen effectively.
>
> Along with a number of practical matters that occur in our lives, there are embedded in all of our psyches many feelings, attitudes, prejudices, and assumptions that pose barriers to effective listening. To overcome them you must acknowledge that you, along with everyone else, harbor attitudes, feelings, and prejudices that affect your conduct and your ability to listen effectively.
>
> We must acknowledge that there are times when we don't care, and have no interest in listening. As long as we have considered the consequences of not listening and have concluded that it doesn't matter, there is probably no reason to waste energy listening and trying to assimilate what the speaker has to say.

- Look that person in the eye. Eye contact is very important!
- Slightly extend your hands, and open your body in a receiving way.
- Ask, "Is this a good time to talk? I'm ready to listen."

The methodology of what I call the Relax and Focus technique and the research documenting its benefits are set forth in *The Relaxation Response* by Herbert Benson, MD. This book made a big difference in my life. Many friends to whom I have recommended it have expressed gratitude. If you don't have time to read it in its entirety before going into a situation where you know that you will feel anxious, threatened, or intimidated, read pages 159 through 163, as far in advance as possible.

While this Relax & Focus technique is especially well-suited to formal relationships, a more informal approach may be effective under other circumstances.

Step Two: Spot Those Listening Barriers

- Distraction, desire, or compulsion to be doing something else
- Anxiety, embarrassment, impatience, or nervousness

Master These Listening Techniques   7

- Attitudes, assumptions, and prejudices
- Lack of interest, ignorance, or apathy
- Preparing to respond
- Too busy or don't want to listen

Step Three: Hurdle Those Listening Barriers

Distraction, desire or need to be doing something else. If listening is essential, verbally acknowledge your state of distress. Relax and Focus (R&F), and take a moment to work through it. Inform the speaker that you want to hear what they have to say and that you want to take notes and play back your understanding of what is said.

Anxiety, embarrassment, impatience, or nervousness. Whether you know the cause of your tension or not, verbally acknowledge it, without explaining the reason. R&F. take a moment to work through your tension. Inform the speaker that you want to hear everything s/he has to say and that you want to take notes and play back your understanding of what s/he has said.

Attitudes, assumptions, and prejudices. You may react unfavorably to a speaker based on his/her appearance, behavior, accent, ethnicity, job title, or your prior experience with him/her. You may lack respect for, feel intimidated by, or be uncomfortable with the speaker. R&F. Acknowledge and recognize your feelings. Try to separate the message from the messenger. R&F. Smile, make eye contact, and adopt an open, receptive body language.

Lack of interest, ignorance, or apathy. (When asked "What is the difference between ignorance and apathy?" the wag responded: "I don't know and I don't care!") If you need the information or your relationship with the speaker dictates that you have to listen, there is no graceful retreat. If you have a "don't know and don't care" attitude, you must recognize and acknowledge it. Increase your interest level by framing questions as you listen. Taking notes, if appropriate, will also help.

Preparing to respond. The most pervasive listening barrier is the compulsion to prepare a response to what the speaker is saying as soon as you grasp the slightest inkling of where s/he is going with the subject. You may jump to a conclusion this way. In addition to distracting you from what is being said, your facial expressions and your body language will reveal to the speaker that you are thinking about your response, not focusing, and not listening. This can disrupt the speaker's thought process and the flow of conversation as well. Acknowledge and recognize this compulsion. Comedian Georgie Jessel once observed: "If I am laughing when someone tells a joke, it's not his joke I'm laughing at. I'm laughing at the joke I'll tell as soon as he's finished." This may work for Mr. Jessel, but the rest of us must refrain from composing a response. R&F. Try to summarize in your head what is being said so that you can play it back to the speaker when s/he is finished talking.

Too busy or don't want to listen. If you are very busy and do not have time to listen immediately, inform the speaker: "I am a little distracted, but I really want to hear what you have to say. Just give me one minute to make a note of what I have to do and clear my head." R&F. If you cannot or do not want to listen, be kind and courteous. Say: "I hope you will understand, I really cannot listen to you right now." Don't complain and don't explain. Do not set a date for a listening event and create false expectations. If you are confronted with the same person again and you still feel the same way, deal with it at that moment in the same way. If the person responds, "You never have time to listen to me!" Just say, "I am sorry, but I just can't listen to you right now."

Step Four: Did I Really Understand?

When you're sure the speaker is finished, tilt your head and wait for a few seconds. Then, before giving your reaction, say, "Let me be sure I understand what you said." Then play back a summary of the comments. This accomplishes a number of positive things:

- shows the speaker you were listening and heard what was said
- provides an opportunity for the speaker to immediately clear up any misunderstanding
- shows you wanted to hear and understand what was said
- avoids the that's-not-what-I-said-you-never-listen-to-me-you-just-don't-understand-me debate when the subject comes up again

At this point, the speaker will either clarify the comments or acknowledge that you heard and understood what was said. This helps ensure understanding by "buying into your understanding." This cannot be overemphasized. It enables the speaker to recall saying: "Yes, you did understand what I said," if the issue comes up later. This is true even if the speaker has had a change of heart in the interim. Using such a technique will avoid a response like that old saying: "I know you believe you understand what you think I said, but I'm not sure you realize that what you heard is not what I meant!"

Also, by communicating to the speaker that you think what he or she has to say is important and that you want to understand, you enhance his or her self-esteem and leave the speaker with positive feelings about you.

There will be times when you have not had time to anticipate or prepare for a difficult and uncomfortable situation. If it is not totally inappropriate, say, "I'm a little nervous, I really want to understand what you said." Either play back what you heard or ask that they repeat it. Seldom will the other person or persons have a negative reaction to such a statement. Most people will be sympathetic and understanding. The tension that you are experiencing and communicating through your body language and facial expressions will be relieved. You, and those present, will be more relaxed. The release of tension will improve your ability to listen and understand what is being said, and enable you to communicate more effectively.

Write It Down

If possible have pen and paper ready before you listen. This will demonstrate that:

- you are prepared to listen
- you think the information is important enough to write it down
- you are focused on what is being said.

Taking notes may not be possible or even appropriate in many situations. For example, if a friend is pouring out his or her heart about a difficult personal or family problem, or a health issue, it would be inappropriate and awkward to take notes. But, if the conversation moves to how you can help, then it might be appropriate to say, "Let me jot this down. I want to be sure I get it right," or some other

---

The Bedtime Snack

"Where are you going?" asked a wife as her husband left their bed in the middle of the night.

"To get a glass of milk," he responded.

"Bring me some ice cream," she said. Write it down or you'll forget it!"

"For gosh sake, you want some ice cream. I'll remember."

"Write it down," she insisted, adding, "Put some chocolate syrup on it. Write it down!"

"I'll remember," he said.

"Put some crushed nuts on top too. Write it down."

"Don't be silly," he responded.

The husband went downstairs, had a glass of milk, let the dog out, enjoyed the warm night air and gazed at the stars. Then he remembered that his wife wanted something.

He looked in the refrigerator and found half a hamburger that she didn't finish at dinner. He put it in the microwave, added fresh lettuce, and headed for the bedroom with a satisfied smile on his face.

She looked at the dish and exclaimed, "I told you to write it down!"

"What's the matter?" he asked.

"You forgot the ketchup!"

comment that fits the circumstances and your relationship with the speaker and explains the note taking.

Lots of important listening occurs, or could occur, in momentary exchanges on the run. Your reaction to the "take notes" suggestion might be, "I can't spend my whole life with pad and pen poised." My solution is to carry a card in my shirt pocket. I buy cards with rounded corners that won't punch holes in my shirt. You can get them at printers or possibly at stationery stores. I am never without a pen. It's not necessary to take verbatim notes. Just write down key words to enable you to recall what is said.

There are social or cultural barriers that make it difficult to take notes in many situations. Someone may worry, or even take offense, if you start writing notes without any explanation. You may need to say something that will make the speaker comfortable with your taking notes. Comments such as, "These are important points that I want to remember. Hope you don't mind if I jot down some notes so I won't forget what you're saying." Something along this line should relieve concern and may actually compliment the speaker.

Hearing Impairment As A Listening Barrier

Many individuals develop some hearing loss as they grow older. I am amazed at the numerous friends and family members who refuse to acknowledge that they have hearing loss and, even worse, the severity of the loss. The result is, depending on the degree of impairment, that they either miss a lot of what is being said, or they drive their friends and family crazy asking them to constantly repeat things, or both!

If the impairment is such that hearing aids will not help, then the individual has to work around the impairment by making sure those with whom s/he needs to communicate understand the scope of the limitation. Then, various appropriate techniques can be used such as, speaking louder,

Master These Listening Techniques

more slowly, more clearly, and in extreme cases writing down what needs to be communicated.

But if the impairment can be overcome or at least helped by a hearing aid, by all means do so. Don't deprive yourself of the pleasure of the company of others by denying the problem or succumbing to vanity. I have seen very serious irritation develop between spouses, family members, and friends because someone close to them either denies a hearing problem or refuses to wear a hearing aid.

The more difficult issue is how best to encourage a friend or family member to use a hearing aid. My suggestion is to say something like:

"I really care for you and enjoy your company, your wit, your insights, and the many things you have to offer in our communication. I find myself becoming frustrated and even irritated due to our frequent misunderstandings because of your understandable discomfort about using a hearing aid. I really want to enjoy your company and communicate effectively. I'm concerned that unless you do something about your hearing problem we will just have more frustrations, miscommunications, and misunderstandings. Why don't you check

---

A sixty-five year old man went to the doctor.

"Doc, I'm very concerned about my wife. She doesn't respond when I talk to her."

"Well, that could be any one of a number of problems. But, hearing loss is a common problem at your and her age. Here's what I suggest. When you go home, stand on the other side of the room and say something in a normal voice. If she doesn't respond, go to the middle of the room and say the same thing in a normal voice. If she still doesn't respond, go right up close to her and repeat what you said."

"Okay, Doc. I'll give it a try."

The man went home and immediately followed the doctor's instructions.

"Honey, I heard about a new restaurant that has great food and it's very inexpensive. Would you like to go out to dinner tonight?"

His wife did not respond. So he moved to the middle of the room and repeated the question. Again, she did not respond. So he walked up to her and stood about a foot away, and raising the volume a bit asked her again.

She turned around, looked at him, and said in her loudest voice, "For the third time, yes!"

with some of your friends and other members of the family and see what they think."

This approach communicates that you care, that you are sympathetic, that you are frustrated because the mutual pleasure of each other's company is greatly reduced, that this is a common, correctable, physical problem, and that s/he should verify the problem by checking with others s/he respects. In approaching it this way, you are not complaining or accusing the person of being unreasonable. You are making the person aware of the benefits to be derived from doing something about the problem.

It is obvious that you cannot be a good listener if you can't hear and understand what is being said.

Chapter 2

PRACTICE, PRACTICE, PRACTICE!

A wise commentator recently observed: "You can't lose weight by buying and reading a diet book!" Obvious! Yet, how often we do just that. We buy a book to "help" us do something or do it better, we take the time to read the book, but then we never put into practice what we have learned.

With sports and games, we would never assume that we could just watch someone play golf or tennis and then grab a club or a racquet and be able to play those games like a pro. On the contrary, we probably read a book, take classes, and then practice – maybe for years – in order to become even reasonably competent.

The poet, Samuel Rogers was taciturn and had an acerbic wit. His friend Knight talked a lot and was a terrible listener. When Rogers heard that Knight seemed to be going deaf and could barely hear, he reportedly said: "It's from lack of practice!" You may not go deaf if you don't practice your listening skills, but you will not become a good listener without practice.

The bottom line: you can't lose weight by reading a diet book and you cannot improve listening skills unless you devote the time and effort to learning, applying, and practicing listening skills.

Listen To Yourself

THIS MAY BE THE MOST IMPORTANT POINT IN THIS BOOK! If you can learn to listen to yourself, and, if you practice it, along with the other techniques described in this book, you will probably be a better listener in all situations.

Albert Camus observed, "An intellectual is someone whose mind watches itself."

We all know someone who immediately engages you before you can say hello. He or she launches into a stream-of-consciousness monologue, with every thought that pops into the mind popping out of the mouth. When the conversation is over (meaning when they pause for a breath and you move on), they have no idea what they have said.

IF A PERSON DOES NOT LISTEN TO HIMSELF WHY SHOULD YOU LISTEN TO HIM? TURNING THAT AROUND, IF YOU DON'T LISTEN TO YOURSELF, WHY SHOULD YOU EXPECT ANYONE TO LISTEN TO YOU?

Of course, Henny Youngman would say, "How do I know what my opinion is until I hear what I say?"

You had a terrible time with your kids today. They were out of control, wouldn't listen to you (you should have read them this book!), and did some outrageous things. Your spouse comes home from work, walks in the door, and you say, "I'm exhausted, fed up, and at my wit's end. The kids were awful today. We have to do something about them and you've got to help me!"

Looks like a difficult evening ahead.

How does that approach sound to you? Is it a constructive framework for dealing with the problem?

One approach that might work, "I know you don't like to have problems dumped on you when you come home from work. You've probably had a hard day. But, I had a serious problem with the kids today, and I hope we can talk about it tonight. Let me know when would be a good time to talk about it."

If you had composed your thoughts, rehearsed the words in your head, and listened to yourself, which of the two approaches would be preferable? Which will lead to a more pleasant evening and a possible resolution of the problem?

But, you say, a lot of my give and take with others is on the run. I don't have the luxury of composing something in my head, playing it back, and listening to it before I say it. Yes, it does sound too structured and cumbersome, but we're not talking about a carefully rehearsed Shakespearean scene! If you practice pausing for a split second, and then listening to yourself before you make a point or responding, you will be able to think through your ideas and compose them as you speak.

Listening to yourself is a skill that requires a time commitment in order to perfect and practice the technique.

There are, in most of our lives, times during most days when we are doing something so routine we don't have to think about it. It may be driving the route that we drive every day, raking leaves, jogging, putting out the garbage, or listening to elevator music while waiting for a human to answer the phone; the many moments that we are not engaged with others and have time to reflect. Use some of those moments to focus on some difficult situation that you have to deal with. Think about the person who you will be talking to. Consider why the situation is difficult. Is it the other person, the problem, or both? Think through what you might say. Play it back to yourself and listen. How does it sound? What kind of response will your comments provoke? Would a different approach be better?

When you settle on the approach that you feel best fits the problem and the person with whom you are dealing, play it back to yourself, and, when you have a moment, write it down.

You will not always have the luxury of rehearsing the scenario, writing it down, and reflecting on it. But, if you practice the **COMPOSE, PLAYBACK, LISTEN, AND REFLECT ROUTINE,** you will be pleasantly surprised at how quickly you can put the process into action on the spur of the moment when you are confronted with difficult and awkward situations where you do not have the luxury of pausing, reflecting, composing your thoughts, playing them back to yourself, and editing them.

If you're going to have successful relationships with those you love, with friends, and with people you have to deal with in your job or profession, developing and practicing techniques of listening to yourself may be essential. The approach you choose will depend on the subject matter and your relationship with the other party. It may be a friend, your boss or a fellow worker. You need to think through the best approach for stimulating a constructive response.

Too often, these situations occur at the worse possible moments; such as times when you are in a state of maximum stress. It's time to resort to the Relax & Focus Mode. To indulge a cliché, it's time to "walk a mile in the other persons shoes." (Heard a witty observation about that maxim: "Walk a mile in the other person's shoes. That way you will be a mile away and you will have his shoes!).

I'm not talking about the light conversation that occurs at social gatherings where everyone is talking at once, situations where you are moving from one person to another or dinners in a party atmosphere. In those settings everyone expects humor and spontaneous comments. Spontaneity is a main component of such occasions. But let's assume that you're having a conversation in which it's important to reach a mutual understanding about something. You may be dealing with a serious financial problem, merely working out details of transportation for the kids, planning a vacation, or coping with the myriad logistics which make up our lives. **YOU MUST LEARN TO COMPOSE YOUR THOUGHTS, LISTEN TO THEM, REVIEW THEIR TONE AND CONTENT AND, IF NECESSARY, REVISE THEM BEFORE LETTING THE WORDS OUT OF YOUR MOUTH.**

I once wrote a piece about the debate over our national budget, which included an analysis of issues that are usually ignored. A friend liked the piece and asked: "How long does it take you to write something like that?" I immediately responded, "It took me about a half-hour to forty five minutes once I sat down at the computer." He looked at me with skepticism. "You wrote that piece in little over half an hour! That's hard to believe!"

"Well," I responded. "You have to understand that I run a mile and a half every morning. I write while I'm running to take my mind off the misery. Most of my writing is in my head. When I sit down at the computer, I transcribe the composition, and then I revise, revise, and revise."

Your head is always full of thoughts, ideas, and conversations you want to have or intend to have. The difference is that when you are having an actual conversation and are composing responses and listening to yourself, it must be a focused and disciplined process. Consider recent conversations you have had that did not go as well as you wished. Think through your role. Ask whether you would have had more success if you had listened to yourself before you spoke.

You may still be concerned with the difficulty of trying to compose, listen, and revise in your head when someone is in front of you waiting for a response. There is a solution. **BUY TIME!** Say: "That's an important point, let me think about that for a moment." You may recall that in press conferences, President Nixon never directly responded to a question. He would say, "I am glad you asked that question," or "That's an important question and I want to make sure everyone understands the complexity of that issue." As his staff later explained, this was his method of "buying time" while he composed his answer.

There are a lot of "buy time" devices. You will need to develop techniques with which you are comfortable. "Let me be sure I understand your point or your question, "Would you mind repeating what you just said." This one works for a number of reasons. It gives you time to compose and listen to your response and it lets the other person know that you want to understand what he or she has to say.

You must practice these techniques. But you do not need another person present. Visualize situations with your kids, spouse, friends, or fellow workers, and review some difficult conversations that you have had. I can always think of what would have been the perfect thing to say to someone, after they are no longer present and the situation is past. The French call this "l'esprit de l'escalier," "the wit of the staircase." It refers to the hostess wearily climbing the staircase after a party, her mind flooded with all the witty rejoinders she should have made at key points during the evening.

Many years ago I became aware that at dinner parties or small gatherings one of my closest friends would float an idea or a question to focus conversation. It always appeared spontaneous. Observing him repeat this device at our frequent gatherings, I realized that it was a well thought out technique that was very effective in stimulating interesting conversation. It did not inhibit spontaneity at all. He had obviously composed the thoughts in his head and rehearsed them before the gathering. He was a master of the technique of listening to himself, and I have used his technique to good advantage many times.

EFFECTIVE LISTENING TECHNIQUES ARE LEARNABLE SKILLS. Composing complete thoughts in your head, listening to them, reflecting on them, and perfecting them – these are all learnable skills. But, to make them work for you, you must practice, practice, practice!

How Do I Persuade People To Listen To Me?

Not only must you learn to listen to yourself; you must also learn how to persuade others to listen to you! Here are a few ways to do just that:

1) Make sure they are ready to listen. Ask them: "I want to talk with you about something. Is this a good time?" This shows that you respect the other person's time and highlights the fact that what you want to say is important enough to set aside a time for them to really listen to you.

    This point is important any time and critically important if you are calling someone on the phone. It amazes me how many people call and launch into a subject without asking if I have time to cope with what they have to say. They are calling on their schedule and have no idea what I am doing when I answer the phone. I may be having a heart attack, administering CPR to my wife, trying to write down an inspirational thought, or taking a shower. How easy it is to ask: "Is this a good time, there's something I want to discuss with you." Easy, but how few people employ this courtesy when calling.

    If all else fails, if no one will listen to you, you've tried all of the techniques in this book, and nothing works, there is one approach that will always get their attention and make them listen. Just look them in the eye and say, "I have some scandalous, shocking information about one of our friends. But I can tell you about it only if you take an absolute pledge of secrecy and agree to never divulge this to anyone else!" This is guaranteed to get their attention.

Hopefully such a ruse will not be necessary. There are many other ways to get people to listen to you.

2) Ask for help. When I started practicing law I always seemed to be behind and in a rush. I assumed that those who worked in the County Clerk's office, where legal documents had to be filed, were there to serve me. I would dash in, throw documents on the counter, and say, "Please file these right away. I'm in a rush."

My insensitivity and lack of respect for their job blew up in my face. I soon learned that those behind the counter at the County Clerk's office could be more formidable opponents and barriers to success than any opposing counsel. They could find technical flaws in whatever was presented to them and could create serious problems if they were not treated with dignity and respect.

One day when I desperately needed to have something filed before a critical deadline I approached one of the older clerks who had always smiled and had been helpful despite my youthful impatience, and said "Kay, I really need your help. I have to file this before 5 p.m., or else I'm in deep trouble. Can you please help me?"

She smiled, and said, "Of course I'll help you Charlie. Tell me what you need."

She got the job done. As I drove back to the office the significance of what had just happened filtered through my head. Rather than stalking in, demanding service, and treating the clerks as if they were my personal servants, I had asked for help, acknowledged the importance of their knowledge and experience, and dignified their job. It was something they deserved but seldom heard.

This lesson served me well. First I realized that if you treat people in service positions with disrespect and trivialize their job because you are focusing only upon your own needs, it is rude, insensitive, and designed to create big problems for you. Even good-natured individuals who are devoted to their jobs and want to help can become obstreperous if treated with disrespect. Individuals who are obstreperous by nature can become impossible and make your life miserable if not treated with courtesy and respect.

Stating that you need help and asking someone to help you avoids the appearance of being demanding and arrogant and usually makes the person with whom you are dealing feel worthwhile and feel that what they do is important. And, if you need their services – especially if their action or failure to act can be costly to you – it *is* important to you.

Some learn this lesson the hard way and at great expense. A big shot partner of a national consulting firm came to small town USA and tried to impress a local property tax assessor with his expertise. He played games with what he considered a local rube. The expert who was infected with a number of listening barriers ended up costing his clients well in excess of a million dollars.

It was a very expensive exercise in failing to listen.

3) Don't believe everything you hear. Large and small companies hire individuals to handle phone inquiries and complaints. The usual practice is to provide these individuals with canned general answers to inquiries and complaints. They are instructed that if the caller wants to know the background or the reason for the

answer, they are told to respond, "That's our standard policy" or "That's our standard rate." The message is clear; everyone, rich or poor, is treated the same way. This policy is standard and we don't vary from it.

My wife and I planned a trip to Europe. She had a serious physical handicap and I didn't want to go unless we could fly Business Class. But, on an international flight that costs an arm and a leg and your children's inheritance. I have a very special travel agent who is a good friend and a genius at finding good fares. I called and said, "Help."

She said: If you have an American Express Platinum card you can get a free ticket in business class. I said I don't even have an American Express charge card. "Get a Platinum card and call me back," she said.

I called American Express. "I'm sorry," explained the customer service person. "You can only get a Platinum card if you are an American Express card holder, and even then it is by invitation only. That's our standard policy."

I didn't believe it. So, after speaking with two sets of supervisors and finally the person in charge of the Platinum department, I got the card in ten days, notwithstanding the non-variable "Standard Policy."

When confronted with the "Sorry, that's our standard policy," response you must realize that the person you are talking to has no authority to alter the policy or give you any encouragement. In a polite way, tell the phone person that you are not challenging them, that you realize they are just doing their job, and that you appreciate their courtesy. But you need to say, without apologizing, "There are some special circumstances here and I need to speak to a supervisor."

I have never been turned down when I ask to speak to a supervisor. On every occasion that I have by-passed the "standard policy" response I have had a good response to my request. I don't ask for any treatment that I would not be willing to give were I in the supervisor's position.

4) Be persistent but polite. When my mom was only fifty-five, her hypochondria inspired her to buy a crypt in a local facility because she wanted to be buried with the rest of her family. She paid 350 hard-earned dollars for the crypt. A few days before she died at age 93, I called the crypt company to alert them that the funeral home would be delivering my mom's casket within a week.

I was informed that there would be an "Opening and Closing fee." The fee would be $500 if the casket was delivered on a weekday or $750 if delivered on the weekend. I informed the manager that I had her contract before me and that there was no mention of an opening or closing fee and that I would not pay one. "I'm sorry," he said. "That's our standard policy and we never waive that fee!"

"When she dies the casket will be delivered to your facility. I expect you to put the casket in the crypt. There will be no opening or closing fee paid."

"I can't waive the fee he said. Maybe you better speak to our general counsel."

The General Counsel was very pleasant and firm. I informed him that since his company prepared the form contract and there was no mention of an opening and closing fee no judge would support their position. "I want the fee waived," I said in a polite but firm voice.

"I can't do that without talking to our management," he said. "I'll hold" I responded. Less than 30 seconds later he came back on the phone and informed me that they had "agreed" to waive the fee.

"Standard Policies" enforced by polite, tough, well trained, phone receptionists are effective barriers which protect companies and their key personnel from people who think that they are entitled to be treated fairly and as individuals.

You can get over these barriers if your circumstances are unusual or unique and your requests are reasonable. But, you must be courteous and understand the role and responsibility of the phone person when asking to speak to a supervisor. Don't explain your special circumstances to the phone person. It's useless. Tell the phone person that your circumstances are unusual and that you need to talk to a supervisor. Tell the supervisor that you need help and that you are confident that he or she can help you. It has worked like a charm for me. The important point is to get the supervisor to deal with you as an individual with specific problems. You must distinguish yourself from those hordes that threaten the peace and solitude of management. Use a little charm, ask for help, and make the supervisor feel that you are not yet another one of those individuals that he or she has to get rid of.

In the past few years I have been successful in obtaining relief from every supervisor to whom I have spoken. (I suppose if very many people read this book, companies will have to hire a lot more supervisors!)

One last amusing anecdote. When I made the phone call to the crypt company I was in the room of my mom's sister, my ninety-year-old aunt. She overheard the entire conversation. She's amazing, can out-walk me, and is very funny. When I hung up, she chuckled, looked at me, and said, "I have a crypt at the same place. I hope you will handle my delivery when I pass on!"

Chapter 3

LISTEN AT WORK

"Nobody ever listened himself out of a job."
Calvin Coolidge

Listening is just one part – one very big part – of the communication process. And in the workplace, effective communication is critical to every aspect of a successful business. It all starts with listening.

When I went to law school there were no courses in how to listen effectively. The assumption was, if you are smart enough to be here and get through law school, you must know how to listen. My experience and a Washington Post article about doctors who do not listen, belie that assumption.

There were also no courses in training and supervising beginning lawyers. When our law-practice expanded, we hired lawyers just out of law school. I had to train and supervise these bright young people with exceptional educations, who had no knowledge or experience in how to be an effective lawyer. Problems kept occurring. There was confusion about assignments and my expectations. Unnecessary and non-billable work was being done. This confusion and miscommunication produced mutual dissatisfaction between me and the employees. I realized that either I was not communicating well, the employees were not listening well, or both.

I gave the problem a lot of thought. I talked to some of my partners and to some of the associates with whom I had

> This verbatim excerpt from a court transcript demonstrates what can occur when a lawyer does not listen in the courtroom:
> Defendant: Judge, I want you to appoint me another lawyer.
> Judge: And why is that?
> Defendant: Because the Public Defender isn't interested in my case.
> Judge (to public defender): Do you have any comments on defendant's motion?
> Public Defender: I'm sorry, Your Honor, I wasn't listening.

developed good relationships. And I worked out a system that proved to be very effective. I prepared a memorandum that I gave to each employee that came under my supervision. They were instructed to keep this handy and refer to it whenever they received an assignment from me. (I also gave them an article that I cherish about "How to Deal With Difficult People.")

The memorandum informed them that if they failed to understand assignments, even though the failure to understand might be inadequate instructions from me, it was their job and career at risk. Therefore it was essential for their own self-interest to follow a system of clarifying the assignment and the scope of the task that was failsafe. The memorandum contained the instructions for dealing with every assignment.

The use of this procedure accomplished the following:

1) It clarified at the outset any miscommunication between me and the employee. Once I read the memorandum, cleared up any misunderstanding, and signed off on it, I could not later claim that the employee didn't understand my instructions. By signing off on the employee's understanding of the assignment and how and when it was supposed to be done, I had bought into that understanding.

2) It enabled the law firm to identify, early on, lawyers who either could not understand assignments or who could not produce acceptable results.

This approach, while designed for training and supervising new lawyers, is easily adaptable to other work situations. I have passed this tool along to a number of individuals who have been promoted to positions with training and supervisory responsibilities. I have had many positive reactions from those who have utilized the technique.

I have also passed it along to a number of individuals who were having problems dealing with their supervisors. An employee who is having trouble with a boss can adapt and use this technique in specific job situations. This process can enable the employee to understand his or her own problems in listening and understanding or to identify that they are working for a supervisor who cannot communicate effectively. Actually, the technique is useful even if there is a good relationship between the boss and the employee. The technique can avoid mistakes and misunderstandings in even the best of relationships.

> When an assignment is received, before doing anything else, prepare a memorandum setting forth your definition and understanding of the assignment including the following:
> 1. Define the final product that you are expected to produce. For example, it could be a research memorandum, draft of a contract, filing of a lawsuit, etc.
> 2. Describe your understanding of the time line for completing the assignment, and the priority of that assignment among your other projects.
> 3. Explain your understanding of the methodology for completing the project and the tasks you need to perform to complete the project. For example, you may need to gather additional facts, do research, contact the client, etc. Before contacting the client or anyone outside of the office, check with me first.
> 4. Itemize any additional information or instructions you need from me in order to proceed with the project.
> Your memorandum does not have to be formal. It can even be in your own handwriting. The important thing is to do it promptly, return it to me, and clear up any misunderstandings between us before you spend time on the project.

The technique has to be adapted to fit the situation and the time constraints of the job. While it is safer to have the understanding in writing, it will not always be possible to do that in the dynamics of the workplace. But even an oral verification will highlight the effort to "be sure that I understand the project" and will in most cases be remembered by the boss.

Ask Skillful Questions

In the workplace, information gathering is key to the problem-solving process, as well as to the interview process, each of which revolves around the ability to frame skillful questions that elicit a direct and concise response. In order to produce such answers, you must frame a question that can be answered as directly as it was asked. It must be a concise question, not mere rumination.

For example, a department supervisor says to her boss, "It's been weeks since we've had a departmental staff meeting. All the employees want to have one. The last time we did this was when we took that long lunch hour and ordered in pizza. I don't know when we can get everyone together for lunch like that again. But we have to get together. I don't know what to do to make this happen."

What exactly is the question here? How about a different approach.

"The employees would like a staff meeting. It has been three months since the last one. I have checked everyone's schedules, including yours, and here are some dates that look good. We can have a morning meeting in the conference room, or we can have a long lunch and order in pizza like last time. Which date works best for you, and which alternative would you prefer?"

Think through the problem and define the question. Frame the question so that it can be answered directly and concisely. Listen to yourself. Determine whether there is a question and whether you could answer it. This will get to a solution and avoid frustration and a waste of time and energy.

And if the one who is attempting to frame a question can only produce a rumination or a worry, then it is up to the listener to reframe the question. A playback that might work is, "Shall we check out all our calendars and pick a date? Do you want to have a pizza lunch again? If so, can you let me know a date, and I'll have my secretary send everyone a memo advising them of the date and time. She'll also take care of ordering the pizza. What do you think about doing it that way?

This demonstrates that you are listening and are prepared to deal with the problem that is of concern to the speaker.

As you can see, listening to and responding to questions involves two different issues:

1) Listening to the question and, if necessary, seeking clarification, and responding in a way that is not provocative and which answers the question, if you know the answer. And if you don't know the answer, acknowledging your lack of knowledge and if necessary agreeing to seek an answer.

2) Listening to responses to your questions, being sure that your question was fully understood. If the response does not deal with the question, try to determine whether the response is a diversionary tactic or whether the question was not understood. Bring the respondent back to the issue. This can be done by either re-framing the question or seeking to understand, in a non-confrontational manner, whether the respondent understood the question. One possibility, "Let me just be sure you understood my question, because I'm a little confused by your response."

Most everyone is familiar with the old conundrum, "Why did the chicken cross the road?" An amusing treatment of this ancient item has circulated on the Internet in various forms, and my reworked version appears here.

> Q. WHY DID THE CHICKEN CROSS THE ROAD?
>
> A. DR. SEUSS: Did the chicken cross the road? Did he cross it with a toad? Yes! The chicken crossed the road, but why he crossed, I've not been told!
>
> A. GRANDPA: In my day, we didn't ask why the chicken crossed the road. Someone told us that the chicken crossed the road, and that was good enough for us.
>
> A. ARISTOTLE: It is the nature of chickens to cross the road.
>
> A. KARL MARX: It was an historical inevitability.
>
> A. CAPTAIN JAMES T. KIRK: To boldly go where no chicken has gone before.
>
> A. FOX MULDER: You saw it cross the road with your own eyes. How many more chickens have to cross before you believe it?
>
> A. FREUD: The fact that you are at all concerned that the chicken crossed the road reveals your underlying sexual insecurity.
>
> A. EINSTEIN: Did the chicken really cross the road or did the road move beneath the chicken?
>
> A. BILL CLINTON: I did not cross the road with THAT chicken. What do you mean by chicken? Could you define chicken, please?
>
> A. GEORGE W.: That was no chicken. It was a rooster dressed like a chicken. It crossed that road to ravish 5 of Texas' finest hens. It was a fowl act! That rooster was convicted by a jury of its poultry. His guilt was established by irrefutable DNA evidence. I will not grant a reprieve to that rooster! The scheduled execution will go ahead! We'll feed the remains of that rooster to Al Gore in November!
>
> A. DALAI LAMA: The chicken crossed the road to be one with the other side.

In Life's Essential Interviews - Listen

Every business and most individuals become involved with interviews from time to time. Interviews can take the form of anything from an employment interview to interviewing a new client to determine their needs, to gaining admission to a school, to interviewing a prospective tenant. The

underlying purpose of all interviews is the same: to obtain sufficient information to help make a decision(s).

Interviews involve two (or more) individuals: the interviewee, who is seeking a job or an executive position; and the interviewer, who is engaging in a face-to-face inquiry in order to evaluate the interviewee and determine whether he or she is the right person for the position. The process involves not only finding out about the interviewee's education, training, and experience, but also to evaluate his or her personality to determine whether it is compatible with that of the company and its employees. And, if the position requires the interviewee to deal with the public and/or other employees, the interviewer will have to determine whether the applicant possesses the "people skills" to succeed in such endeavors., and whether he or she is a good listener.

Whatever the purpose of the interview, in order for it to be successful, both parties must listen effectively. The failure to listen effectively can produce unpleasant surprises and be costly if it results in a square peg trying to fit into a round hole.

For example; suppose that you are being interviewed for a job that you want and need. The prospective employer says to you: "Tell me about yourself." How do you respond?

Response #1: "Well I was born in Durham North Carolina. My family was poor. My dad was an alcoholic. My mom worked hard and held the family together but she was a very difficult woman. My brother was three years older than I and was Mr. Macho! My mother forced him to take me to the YMCA when he went swimming with his friends. They used to play "Let's dunk Charlie!" That experience left me terrified of water. I never learned to swim."

Whoa! This is not a psychiatric session where you are supposed to free associate. The employer is seeking information about you that is relevant to the performance of the job for which you are applying. Unless you are applying to be a lifeguard or a swimming coach you are providing way too much information, and you are disclosing emotional problems that will probably be a barrier to your being hired. Let's try something else.

Response #2: I graduated from Stanford Law School near the top of the class in a very competitive environment. Even though it was something of a dog-eat-dog environment, I was able to compete successfully and make many friends that have been close throughout my life. I was appointed Managing Editor of the Stanford Law Review. I have had a successful law practice for seven years. If you could tell me more about the specific requirements of the position, the special qualifications you seek, and what your needs and expectations are, then I can respond to your question with more relevant and helpful information about my background and experience.

A good listener should realize that interviewers have specific goals, namely; to find the right person for the job, the apartment, the school, or whatever.

Now, let's assume that you responded with Response #2. How might the interviewer best respond?

Response A: Oh, you went to Stanford Law School.

One of my best friends went there. From what he told me it really was dog-eat-dog. You must be very bright to have done so well. Of course, we are not looking for a lawyer. We do need an executive with good interpersonal relationship skills and management experience. I don't think that your law school training and your experience practicing law is exactly what we need.

It sounds like the interviewer did not listen to your request for more specific information about the requirements of the job. That would have allowed you to provide helpful and relevant information about your background that may very well pertain to the position. Let's consider another possible response.

Response B: That's helpful to know about your legal training and experience. You asked me to tell you about the specific job requirements and our expectations. I will spend a few minutes explaining the unique needs that we have and what we hope that the person we hire can accomplish.

At this point, the interviewer will explain the company's needs and expectations, and then ask: "What in your background, training, and experience can be useful to us in achieving our goals?"

These examples illustrate that both individuals must listen effectively so that each can make skillful inquiries that will enable them to obtain essential information and to provide facts that are relevant and helpful to the other person.

An essential component of listening effectively in an interview is listening to yourself, which was covered in Chapter 2. Had the interviewer and interviewee above listened to themselves in responding as described in the first responses, they would, or should, have recognized that their responses were not going to enable them to accomplish their goals.

Only by listening effectively will either party be able to devise creative and penetrating questions that force the other person to disclose information which is essential to each of them making the right decision about the position being offered.

A skillful interviewer will devise questions and approaches that will enable him to determine how the interviewee responds to stress, how creative the interviewee is in problem solving, the interviewee's sense of humor, sensitivity to others and the interviewee's skills in quickly responding to difficult circumstances and issues. If the interviewee listens effectively, he should be able to identify what the interviewer is attempting to accomplish and frame an appropriate response. The failure to listen effectively may well result in the interviewee revealing things about himself that will be a barrier to being hired or appointed to the position.

An acquaintance of mine used to manage residential property, and as part of her job, she had to interview prospective tenants. She created a list of questions to ask and then listened very carefully to the responses to determine who would make the best tenant. Her questions were specific but open-ended to encourage a comprehensive response. They covered the individual's lifestyle, work experience, previous residences, and general personality traits, because she wanted to know what kind of a person they were, whether they would stay, pay on time, and get along with the other tenants. Whenever a prospective tenant did not answer a questions in sufficient detail, she would simply ask a more specific or more detailed version of the question. In almost twenty years of property management, she discovered early on that running a credit profile was useless. Knowing how to ask the right questions and listening carefully to the responses were the only real keys to finding reliable, long-term, paying tenants, and to maintaining good tenant-tenant and tenant-manager relations. The proof of how well her interviewing worked? In all those years, managing over 100 units, she had only four evictions.

As a lawyer I often found that I had to skillfully probe to obtain all of the facts from my clients. The failure to get the full story and be aware of the bad facts as well as the good aspects of a client's case often results in very unpleasant surprises and possible disaster if unknown facts are suddenly revealed in court.

No one likes to disclose his or her mistakes or things they did that were stupid or inappropriate. So it has often been necessary for me to be creative and frame very skillful questions in order to get the full story. I have had to learn to read between the lines, watch the body language and eyes, and identify the source of discomfort that suggested that there was more to the story than what was being told.

One of the most important things in obtaining information that a person does not want to disclose, is asking non-threatening questions, questions that are not accusatory.

There are a number of ways of approaching this. Suppose you are a lawyer and you want to find out if your client might have been speeding at the time of the accident. Do you ask, "Were you speeding?" No. Do you ask, "How fast were you going?" No. In all likelihood, the client has only a vague approximation of what speed he or she was traveling. If you ask either of these questions and the client answers, he or she then becomes committed to something that might be in error. In most cases they are not lying, just making a guess that becomes carved in stone in their mind.

Try this instead. Say: "Most of us don't pay attention to what exact speed we are traveling at any particular moment because we are doing defensive driving and being alert to what other drivers are doing. So it's unlikely that you know exactly how fast you were going when the accident happened. Police officers can do a pretty good job of determining the speed at the time of the accident by skid marks and damage done by the impact. Often passengers are more aware of the precise speed than the driver because they are not having to watch the road. Do you have any way of knowing approximately how fast you were traveling at the time of the accident? Were there any witnesses who saw the accident and might testify to your speed? What about your passenger, has he or she made any comment about your speed?"

The best test of whether you have listened effectively in an interview is to summarize and play back to the other person what you heard and your interpretation of what was said. If the other person acknowledges that you have heard what they said and understood what they meant, this does a number of things. The person will remember that they verified your understanding of what was said. It will avoid a later dispute over whether you did hear and understand. The other person will probably be impressed that you paid attention and wanted to hear and understand.

If the other person disagrees with your version of what you heard or understood, then it can be clarified and cleared up on the spot, while memories are fresh and before either can deliberately or inadvertently misremember what they said or thought they said.

The summary and playback does not have to be ponderous. It is probably wise to preface the playback with a comment such as: "It would be useful to me to be sure that I heard and understood what you said. Bear with me for a moment while I summarize my understanding." This communicates that you wanted to understand, and it is a non-threatening way to achieve mutual understanding and verification.

Chapter 4

Difficult Listening

There are many situations in which effective listening seems impossible. We have all had to listen to people who ramble on in a disjointed manner; are indecisive; upset or hurt; angry, aggressive, and defensive; can't take (or give) criticism; or merely can't take a compliment. How do you handle difficult listening situations such as these? It's not easy! But here are a few examples of how to listen and respond to them effectively.

The Stream-of-Consciousness Monologue

In most cases the speaker has something he wants to say. He may be nervous, upset, frantic, or experiencing any number of emotional or psychological states that interfere with his ability to form coherent concise thoughts, and articulate them in an understandable way.

Try to distill the essence of what is being said. (This may require the patience of Job.) Play back a concise summary of the statement. If you can do this it will stimulate a positive and friendly response. You will impress the speaker with your willingness to listen and understand. This process is a demonstration that you heard not only the words but, more importantly, what the speaker meant.

If the statement is so incoherent that you are unable to distill a summary, try, "I'm not sure I understood what you said. Let me think about it. We can try again later." Avoid saying: "You are so upset that you're not making sense." This will merely aggravate the problem and prolong the agony.

After playing back a summary of the statement, suppose the speaker responds: "That's not what I said!" or "That's not what I meant!"

Even if there was a tape recording or a transcript of the statement nothing is accomplished by saying, "Yes, it is!" Such a response is guaranteed to launch an argument and divert the conversation into a "No I didn't!" "Yes, you did!" "Did," "Didn't," child's routine.

When confronted with a "That's not what I said (or meant)" response to your summary, try: "I must have misunderstood. Help me out, I want to understand what you are saying."

At this point the speaker will have had the benefit of your summary and your supportive response and may clarify what he means. This process avoids provocation and arguments.

Misplaced Anger

Suppose you are dealing with a person who is irritated and anxious to dump his irritation and frustration on someone. You are not the source of the irritation but you happen to be a convenient target. You may feel sorry about the plight of this individual, but you may not be in a position to do anything but sympathize. His or her complaints may be just a bitching session about a bad experience on an airline, a spat with a spouse; something purely transitory and insignificant. The complaint may have no merit at all. Little can be gained by engaging such a person in conversation. Sympathy for his feelings and something that will create a diversion to another topic may the best approach. "Sounds like you had a tough time. I hope you can work it out. Heard you had a good trip to San Francisco. Haven't been there for awhile. I'd like to hear about it."

If you are the source of the irritation, the problem is very different. The irritation may be justified or based on unreasonable expectations. For example, suppose you hung out a little too long with friends and were late for what your spouse or friend felt was an important event or meeting, and you had committed to be there on time. The irritation is justified and you are on the spot.

There's not much choice here. You screwed up. Admit it. Ask forgiveness and promise to make it up in some way that will be satisfying to the other person. Don't be defensive. If your response is something like "You have to realize that I was with important clients and I couldn't just walk out and tell them that this party was more important than listening to them!" That will just create more problems for yourself. Admitting the screw-up, asking for forgiveness, and agreeing to make it up to the other person will, in most cases, diffuse the situation and help the other person get through their anger and frustration. Let them acknowledge to themselves that everyone screws up. If you remind them of this rather than letting them acknowledge it to themselves, it will merely aggravate their feelings of frustration and anger.

Now suppose you left work in plenty of time to get home and fulfill your promise to be on time. There was a major accident and you sat in traffic, without moving for over an hour. You walk in the door and are whammed with, "I told you that this was a very important event. It is a very important client and a big deal. We are already a half-hour late and you still have to get dressed. I can never depend on you. I'm furious. If I lose this account you are in deep doo-doo!"

Try, "Please, I understand how upset you are. Let me call and explain that there was a major accident that closed the road for over an hour. I think that they will understand. It's all over the news. A big tanker truck spilled fuel on the highway."

Obviously you have been attacked without justification. Your tendency is to say, "Wait just a damned minute. Don't give me a lot of stuff. I've been sitting on a closed highway for more than an hour and walk in here and get slammed as if I'm a criminal. To hell with your clients! If they are more important than I am, why didn't you just go without me!"

It's not easy to do for the other person what they are unable to do for themselves; that is, control their emotions, listen, get the facts, and deal with the situation on the merits. If you have been an insensitive jerk, okay, we can deal with that. But if you have done the best you can and the other person is unwilling to listen and work through the situation on a reasonable basis, it is necessary for you to do it for them. Offering to solve the problem, "I'll call and tell them about the accident," gets across the fact that there was an accident that made it impossible for you to be on time without your being confrontational or defensive.

Impossible Individuals

I know difficult people, very difficult people, borderline impossible people, and impossible people. There are effective and civil ways to deal with each of them. There is an excellent article by David D. Burns, M.D., called "How to Deal with Difficult People," which was excerpted from his book, "The Feeling Good Handbook," and it describes techniques for dealing with difficult people. His suggestions have been of great benefit to me.

But these techniques are for dealing with people who are, even though difficult, still capable of being civil and acting reasonably. One hopes these techniques will work with very difficult people and occasionally with borderline impossible people. But there are individuals who are not going to respond to any form of civil discourse or act reasonably, unless forced to do so. Impossible people who are trapped in a forest of compulsive behavior cannot, in most cases, respond to civil discourse and act reasonably, even though their behavior destroys relationships with virtually everyone with whom they come in contact.

At some point, we have to recognize and deal with the fact that some individuals simply will not act reasonably or respond to civil discourse. On an individual basis we can drive ourselves crazy and sometimes wreck our own lives unless we acknowledge that there are impossible people with whom we cannot have reasonable relationships and resolve problems in a civil way. Extricating ourselves from relationships with impossible people may be painful and  disruptive, but continuing such relationships may be worse.

The obvious solution is to avoid contact with such individuals if possible. But there are times when we have no choice. We have to deal with an impossible person.

In my law practice, in business ventures in which I have been a participant, and in the many boards of companies and non-profit organizations on which I have served, I have had to deal with impossible individuals. They insist that their position is the only logical and reasonable one. They claim that they occupy the high ground when, in fact, they are really on their high horse. They attack and insult anyone who disagrees with them. They frequently get their way because they intimidate other participants, or the other participants become so exhausted that they throw up their hands, give up, and give in.

The first and most important rule for dealing with an impossible person is: Don't engage them, don't respond to their insults or personal attacks, and, never respond in kind by counterattacking.

Address your remarks to the other participants. If you present a well-organized, principled position, with verifiable facts, the other participants will see the wisdom of your position. They will also see the flaws in the position of Mr. Impossible. This will, in most cases, stimulate positive responses and encourage others to join in a constructive discussion and solution.

If you are involved in a one-to-one confrontation with Mr. Impossible, the best alternative is to listen, then buy time. "Let me think about this. I'll get back to you promptly with my reactions," is an effective technique. If Mr. Impossible demands, "We have to decide this issue right now!" Again, buy time and say, "I'm sorry, but I cannot make a decision this minute. I'll get back to you before the day is over."

Write out your ideas in a concise way, pointing out the advantages of your position and the problems that might result if another course of action is taken. Do not attack Mr. Impossible's ideas and certainly don't tell him that he is being stupid and illogical. Stick with the facts and the advantages to be gained by your approach, and the problems that might result if your approach is not followed. Deliver this to Mr. Impossible and agree on a time that you can discuss it after he has had a chance to review it, but not immediately.

I have found that these approaches sometimes enable Mr. Impossible to respond positively and save face by putting his own spin on the proposals submitted to him and making them his own.

If you are in a one-to-one situation with Mr. Impossible, and you have to get a problem resolved immediately, it may be necessary to bring in a third party such as a mediator or even a neutral mutual friend to assist. In most cases, Mr. Impossible feels that everyone else is the problem and this makes it impossible to have constructive dialogue. Bringing in a neutral third person can sometimes bring to his attention that it is he – not the others – who is standing in the way of resolving the problem.

> This "last resort" approach to trying to communicate with an impossible person has been circulating on the internet.
>
> Picture yourself near a stream. Birds are softly chirping in the crisp, cool, mountain air.
> No one knows your secret place. You are in total seclusion from that hectic place called "the world."
> The soothing sound of a gentle waterfall fills the air with a cascade of serenity.
> The water is clear.
> You can easily make out the face of the impossible person you're holding under water.
> There now! Feeling better?

If the problem is serious and financially threatening, there is an expensive technique that has worked on a few occasions in dealing with impossible individuals. Have a lawsuit prepared setting forth the facts. Do not file it, but deliver the document to the other party and inform them that this lawsuit will be filed within 10 days unless you are able to reach a satisfactory resolution of the problem. This is a last resort device but there are times when such steps are necessary in dealing with Mr. Impossible.

Dealing With Emotional Overload

- What a person feels is not within his control. How he handles his feelings, responds, and what action he takes are often within his control. Permitting someone to express feelings makes both participants aware of the feelings and possibly

> **Feelings Are Facts**
>
> People cannot control their feelings. They can refrain from acting out feelings, but they can't "not feel that way!" Feelings are facts! People may be able to work through their feelings but they can't change the way they feel.
>
> Feelings are either suppressed and come out in an unrelated way, or they are acknowledged, expressed, and dealt with as well as possible.
>
> Feelings are not something to be debated. It seldom, if ever, serves a useful purpose to argue that feelings are not justified, even if all the evidence and logic point that way.
>
> Acknowledge feelings, saying, "I understand how you feel," not, "I don't understand how you can feel that way." And, don't say "I understand why you feel that way," because you may not understand the "why."
>
> A few neutral questions can be appropriate and might demonstrate to the speaker that you do want to understand and be sympathetic. Non-challenging questions can help the speaker clarify the feelings and may help the speaker gain insight.

aware of why a person is moody, unhappy, or angry. If a person suppresses his feelings and "pops off" with anger or irritation, a reaction seemingly unrelated to the situation, neither party can identify the source of the anger or irritation. This makes it difficult or impossible to deal with the feelings that give rise to the anger or irritation.

One possible response could be, "I understand how you feel. Is there anything I can do?" In most cases listening, and confirmation that you understand "how" the speaker feels, is enough. But, by adding, "Is there anything I can do?" you deliver a message that says, "I care how you feel and I want to be supportive."

Emotions are not always negative. There are also feelings of enthusiasm or excitement that may seem inappropriate to the circumstances or that you can't understand. The speaker may have said "What a marvelous painting!" referring to a canvas that has turned you off. You feel that the canvas is one upon which the artist must have spilled a bucket of paint. In a play called "Art," three close friends have such conflicting feelings about a painting that it almost destroys their friendship. One of the characters pays a large sum for a white-on-white painting. His two closest friends think the painting is a joke. One friend, understanding the emotional and financial investment in the piece, is complimentary and reassuring. The other friend tells the owner that he has been ripped off and was stupid for spending so much for something that looks like a stucco wall. With superb wit and irony, the play masterfully dramatizes the difficult problems of working through conflicting and intense feelings and attitudes among intimates.

Suppose a friend tells you that she is madly in love with her pastor; who is happily married. Your first reaction may be to say "Lassie, get help!" But another approach is probably necessary. It would be helpful to acknowledge that she is in a very difficult situation and needs to give the matter serious thought and talk through it with some wise neutral person who she can trust, maybe you. Non-challenging questions about how and when the feelings came about, whether she feels that the pastor has encouraged her to believe that he has the same feelings about her, and whether she has any ideas of how to work through the situation might help her and enable you to help her pursue a constructive course of action.

Suppose the feelings are anger towards you. If you feel that your conduct or comment triggered – not caused – the feelings, and that the anger is justified, try this response: "I understand how you feel. I'm truly sorry that you are upset about something I said or did." This is neither a guilty plea nor a false acknowledgement that you feel guilty. It is simply a truthful statement that you are sorry that the person feels the way that he or she does.

I was running one morning. A man was walking in the opposite direction with his Rottweiler. The dog was not on a leash, and our area has a leash law. I was afraid the dog might attack me.

"Restrain your dog!" I growled.

"My dog is not bothering you!" he responded.

As I ran and reflected on the situation, I realized that he was right. The dog was not bothering me. I was feeling bothered by the dog. So, you may not have done or said anything inappropriate, but the other person may be, nevertheless, "bothered."

Of course, there is also the distinct possibility that you may recognize that you have done or said something inappropriate and are willing to acknowledge it. In that case, an appropriate reaction might be: "I'm sorry about what I did or said. I hope you will forgive me."

People Who Cannot Accept Compliments

Some people are uncomfortable with compliments and praise. Someone says: "You did a wonderful job, thank you," and they respond with:

Well I could have done a lot better if I had just ...
I should've ...
I am embarrassed that I didn't ...
Next time I will do a lot better ...

The person is seeking reassurance that you really mean what you are saying and wants to hear the compliment again.

Responding this way makes everyone uncomfortable and prolongs an exchange in a never ending "Oh you were wonderful!." "Oh, no, it wasn't very good!" They are pleading for reassurance. The person offering the praise is in a Catch-22. How long must they spend convincing you that you are okay and that they meant what they said?

What if you paused, smiled, and said: "What a kind generous person you are. Thank you. You inspire me to do even better next time!"

The latter response informs the speaker that:

You HEARD what was said.
You understand and appreciate the genuineness of the message
You are not accusing the person of engaging in flattery just to make you feel good.
You acknowledge that they appreciate your effort.

With the "thank you" response, both of you can move on and feel good about the job you have done. Your effort has been acknowledged and is appreciated, and you have LISTENED, heard, accepted, and appreciated the message.

I have a very close friend who I use as a model for gracious acceptance of generosity, whether it is a compliment, a gift, or an offer to share. He is fun to be with. He is someone with whom you can share experiences and good fortune. He accepts with aplomb and genuine gratitude others' generosity. No "Oh you shouldn't have done that!" and no "Oh, gosh, I don't deserve that!" or 'I can't accept that!" He smiles and says, "Thank you, that is wonderful."

In his early 40s he had a tragic accident and became a quadriplegic. His ability to accept help graciously and face life with a smile has enabled him to continue his medical career with great distinction and live a remarkable life as a most delightful individual. He has a rare sense of humor, is interested in everything, is well read, and is without an ounce of hubris or obsequiousness. He is never maudlin. He is a good listener.

Yogi Berra sets an example of how to accept compliments graciously. He relates the story of receiving the Key to New York City from Mayor Lindsay on a miserably hot, humid day. The Mayor's wife, Mary, looked at Yogi's flamboyant outfit and greeted him with, "Yogi, you're looking really cool today!" Yogi replied, "You're not looking too hot yourself!"

Indecisive People - Help Them Decide

We all know individuals who just can't make up their minds. The decision may be as simple as ordering from a menu in a restaurant or as complicated as how to allocate scarce financial resources among essential needs. The process of listening to and dealing with such a person can be painful and frustrating.

It's best to give the indecisive person the freedom to make the decision. You agree to help collect essential information and assist in the process of evaluating the consequences of each alternative. Offer to support whatever decision is made. This process helps avoid arguments and enables you to establish a deadline for the decision and a means of getting the other person off the hook if it is obvious that he or she is unable to reach a decision.

Consider the couple who has saved for a big vacation. The time is here. They have considered every alternative, read, fantasized and talked endlessly. They have finally agreed that it will be ten days in rural France, ten days in the Caribbean, or two weeks in Hawaii. The husband is having a hard time making a decision. His wife is happy with any one of the three.

Wife: "We need to reach a decision and make reservations."
Husband: "I really want to go to France and eat that wonderful food, practice my French and roam around the countryside."
Wife: "Well, it's France."
Husband: "But you know how much Jane and Harry loved the Caribbean. And there is a resort where they speak French and all the chefs are French."
Wife: "Well then, let's go for the Caribbean."
Husband: "But that's such a long trip for only 10 days. I have been under such stress. The thought of being on a beach in Hawaii for two weeks is irresistible!"

How would you deal with this situation?
First, you do as the wife has done, and listen. Then try this:

Wife: "Well, whatever you decide is fine with me. We have to decide by X date in order to make reservations. You think about it and when you decide let me know and I'll make the reservations. If you haven't decided by X, I'll make the decision and make the reservation."
Husband: "Which one will you choose?"
Wife: "It will be a surprise!"

What is happening? The minute the husband makes a decision he suffers over giving up the other two experiences. He feels sorry for himself. He is focusing on the hole and not the donut. Remember the poem posted in every donut shop:

> As you travel on through life, brother,
> Whatever be your goal,
> Keep your eye upon the donut,
> And not upon the hole!

Lots of wisdom in that bit of doggerel.
The story continues. Date X arrives. The wife has made reservations for Hawaii. On the plane, the husband starts whining.

"I think we should have gone to France. I can taste that French food!"
Time to fill the hole in the donut!
Wife: "By the time we were over jet lag going and coming, we wouldn't have had much fun. That will be our next trip, but we'll take three weeks. Anyway, there are some wonderful French restaurants where we're going in Hawaii. You're going to enjoy every minute and be relaxed and refreshed when you get home."

Consider this situation. It is not a dilemma over which trip to take, but one that involves a serious financial issue. The couple has scrimped and saved so they can remodel their kitchen. The appliances are on their last legs and the kitchen doesn't function well. But, the roof is leaking. They probably need a new roof. One of their cars needs major repairs. It will cost lots of money that will never be recovered. They need a new car; reliable transportation for wife to get to work. They can either have a new roof, a remodeled kitchen, or a new car.

In this instance, the wife has the difficulty making decisions. If the kitchen is remodeled, her life will be much easier. She doesn't want to waste money fixing up the old car. She's afraid of what will happen if they don't put on a new roof. She has a problem for every solution. Listen:

Husband: "Why don't we remodel the kitchen, patch the roof, and repair the car."
Wife: " If we remodel the kitchen and the roof leaks it will wreck everything."
Husband; "Okay. We'll do the roof."
Wife: "That means we won't be able to remodel the kitchen for years. The dishwasher won't last that long."
Husband: "We'll do the roof and get a new dishwasher."
Wife: "But the dishwasher won't fit when we remodel the kitchen, and if the car breaks down and I'm late for work, I'll be in trouble with my boss."

The husband needs to write down the choices, put them in front of the wife, and ask her to think about which choice she wants to make, recognizing that neither choice is going to be completely satisfactory. If she wants him to make the decision he will.

Husband: "Winter's coming and we have to make a decision. Let's set a week from today for the final decision. If you

can't decide by then, I'll do what I think is the best."
Wife: "Which one will you pick?"
Husband: "Let me surprise you. I'll do what you want to do, what will make you most comfortable and secure. But we have to make a decision. So if you don't let me know by next week I will go ahead and get it done."

There is obviously no perfect decision. You have listened, avoided an argument, and set up a process for reaching a decision. You have offered to assist them to get the facts and evaluate the alternatives to help the indecisive person make the decision. You have offered to support whatever decision is made. You have established a deadline for the decision. You have offered to make the decision and move on if the other person is unable to decide. There is nothing else you can do.

Handling Criticism

Visionary Stephen Wright says, "For every action there is an equal and opposite criticism."

The most difficult criticism to handle is when the other person is right.

Henny Youngman observed: "For the truth about yourself listen to your enemies."

The Greek philosopher Epictetus, who lived almost 2000 years ago, said, "If someone criticizes you, agree at once. Mention that if only the other person knew you well, there would be more to criticize than that." Follow his suggestion and be amazed at how effectively you disarm your critics.

The minute you hear something that you perceive as criticism, put your sword and shield away and listen, listen, listen! If you can listen without preparing a defense and a counterattack, you might learn something helpful.

A recent study by Ph.D.'s Sybil Carrere and John Gottman found that in carefully controlled experiments with newlyweds, after only three minutes of observation, it is possible to predict who will divorce and who will remain married. One of the most significant predictive factors: defensiveness! In marriages where the husband responded defensively in marital interaction, divorce was very predictable.

Some comments may sound like criticism to you but may not be intended as criticism by the speaker. When it sounds like criticism and your hackles bristle and you prepare to defend yourself, breathe deeply. Rather than raising a wall of defense, turn the situation into a beneficial experience. Treat it as an opportunity to build your own credibility.

Admit mistakes if you recognize any. Show that you want to cooperate, improve, and help your employer, co-workers, friends, or family solve a problem or make a project work.

As our law firm's business expanded it became necessary to hire and train young lawyers. I learned an important lesson from an associate who worked under my supervision. Projects would come back with understandable defects considering his lack of experience and the complexity of the project.

But, I found that he listened carefully to my criticism and suggestions. He asked for explanations if he did not understand something. He never made excuses, argued, or challenged my suggestions. His redrafts came back significantly improved. My suggestions and criticisms, where appropriate, were incorporated with insightful improvements. Suggestions that were not valid, based on additional research and fact finding, were discretely and cogently explained away.

From him I learned about the benefits of purging defensiveness from my personality. He became a key partner in the firm and now has his own firm. His learning curve far exceeded those who had difficulty accepting criticism, and who became committed to their theories and approaches. He was a joy to work with.

He was in sharp contrast to a contemporary associate who was "a bundle of feelings waiting to be hurt." Trying to suggest something to him was like having a root canal. He was bright, dedicated, and ambitious, but impossible to deal with.

Assume your boss comes to you and says that the project proposal you prepared is unacceptable. Your adrenaline surges and you go on the defensive. You knocked yourself out on that project under impossible time pressure. You want to challenge your boss. What will you accomplish other than to strain the relationship? He has made up his mind. What do you do?

Ask for specifics. Don't say, "What was wrong with it?" This can be challenging and provocative. Try, "I hope you don't mind going through the proposal and pointing out the problems so that I can correct them?" As he explains the problems, try to find something you can agree with and acknowledge a problem.

> Boss: "It was much too long and repetitive. No one is going to read all of it. Some of your facts were wrong. And your conclusions don't hold up."
> You: " You're right. It was too long and repetitive. I should have spent more time revising before I gave it to you. I'll do that right away. What facts were not right?"
> Boss: "You said two plus two was five."
> You: "You're right, that doesn't sound correct."
> Boss: "I don't think those statistics are accurate. Where did you get them?"
> Now he has admitted that he is not sure. Don't' argue or try to claim that you know they are right. Instead try this:
> You: "I will double check those statistics. I want to be sure they're accurate. Help me understand the problems with the conclusions."

Difficult Listening

The conclusions may be a combination of facts and opinions. The facts can be verified, but the opinions are going to have to be worked through. If there is any doubt about the facts upon which the conclusions are based, it will be better to find out what it is about the conclusions that bother the boss.

You: "I will double-check the facts and then we can go over the conclusions so that you will be satisfied that the report is a quality product that accomplishes its goals."

This is also an important time to review the goals to be sure that you have a common understanding.

Suppose the boss is dumping on you.

Boss: "You realized that this was an important project. It means a lot of business. If our competitors get the contract we're in big trouble. It was a sloppy job. I can't understand why you turned in such a lousy project."

He is really hurting you now. You can think of a thousand ways to defend yourself. The deadline was ridiculous, you weren't feeling well, your wife had an operation, and you couldn't get any help from your fellow employees.

Rather than getting into a dumping battle that you are sure to lose, try:

You: "At some point I would like to explain why the project did not turn out as well as I would have liked. But the most important thing right now, the top priority, is to get it right. I'll work on it. When it's done and we are both satisfied I want to talk to you about some of the problems I ran into."

When all is done, the boss may be ready to be sympathetic and help you solve the problems you had faced. To sum up this process:

Acknowledge any mistakes.
Don't make excuses. (Don't complain and don't explain.)
Agree to correct errors even if you are not responsible for them.
Ask for an explanation of any problem that you don't understand. Try to get as many specifics as possible without being challenging.
Solicit suggestions for improvement and ways that you might improve your performance and improve your relationship with the critic.
Commit to doing better.
Express appreciation for the time and effort spent by the critic and the suggestions that he made.
Take the time to review the exchange and reflect on your role and how you might use the critical comments to improve yourself.

But suppose the Boss is just having a bad hair day, his comments are dead wrong and, for whatever reason, you are the unfortunate target of his bile. You haven't made any mistakes, you know the proposal will work, and you did your best work because you knew how important it was to the company.

You: "I've taken some notes. Let me be sure that I understand your comments."

Play back a summary of what you heard. Without sarcasm, play back any comments that you know are inaccurate. This may get his attention.

You: "I understand your comments. Let me go over my proposal again and review it with your comments in mind. Can we set a time to discuss it when neither of us will be distracted? I know how important this is to the company."

Whether there are mistakes or the proposal is just great, try to find an opportunity to review the situation with the critic at a time when there is a minimum of stress and tension.

Offering Criticism And Listening To The Response

From time to time each of us have to play the role of critic. If you are a parent or if you have a supervisory position at work, this function may be so routine that you don't even listen to yourself. And, when you don't listen to yourself, you may end up delivering messages that you don't know you're delivering and don't want to deliver.

The goal of criticism or suggestions should be clear to you. Is the message simply, "You screwed up," which will rarely produce positive results, or is it, "There may be a better way of doing a task that will produce a better result?"

Assume you are a manager in the San Francisco office of a company soliciting business from a Los Angeles company. You have to rely on a Los Angeles employee to draft a proposal. It's a big piece of business. You first receive the proposal just before you get on the plane to Los Angeles You realize that it is defective. Joe, who prepared it, meets you at the airport. You have one day to clean up the proposal before you meet with the other side. You are very upset.

You: "Hi, Joe. Thanks for picking me up. This will give us more time to work on the proposal."

This gets across two messages: you appreciate what he has done for you, and the proposal needs work.

Your impulse may be to say, "This proposal is a mess. Where the hell did you get this garbage." While truthful it will be insulting to Joe and it will be difficult to get his cooperation.

Criticize the product and the methodology, <u>not the</u>

person! There is a fine distinction here. The "bundle of feelings waiting to be hurt" individuals will never understand the distinction. Such individuals will perceive any criticism as a personal attack. But there is a difference. For example:

You: "There are problems with the draft. I don't think it will work. We'll work together to revise the proposal and make every minute count so that it meets our goal, which is to get the business."

In this message you have talked about the product, the goals, and the work that needs to be done. You have not personally attacked Joe. In fact you have informed him that you need his help in order to get the business. Rather than treating him as "something the cat dragged in" you have made him feel worthwhile, useful, and needed.

Under which scenario are you more likely to meet your goal?

As you listen to yourself, before delivering criticism or suggestions, ask if the message is directed to the product and the methodology, or does it contain a personal attack on the person receiving the criticism?

After delivering the critique, listen to the tone as well as the content of the response. The facial expression and the body language of the recipient, along with the tone and content of his words, will give you indispensable clues to his reaction, whether the criticism is being assimilated in a useful way or whether the recipient perceives your message as a personal attack. You may have to try different approaches to stimulate a cooperative reaction. Listening will assist you in fashioning a successful approach.

CHAPTER 5

DISCUSSIONS AND ARGUMENTS

I'm a gregarious person. I spend a fair amount of time talking (and hopefully listening effectively!) with family, friends, acquaintances, and people with whom I come in daily contact in banks, stores, and at my former law office. I am fascinated and perplexed at how often people argue over facts; things that can be easily verified.

Someone says, "Babe Ruth struck out more times than any other professional player in the history of baseball." Someone responds, "You're crazy. Why Joe Schmuck struck out twice as many times as the Babe!"

This dispute can be resolved simply and quickly by merely referring to a book on baseball statistics. But that will destroy the fun these two guys are having, accusing each other of being stupid and ignorant and each claiming to know a lot more about baseball than the other.

It's amazing to me how much time people waste arguing over facts. There are so many issues that are matters of opinion. It can be fun reasoning through the issues, getting other's viewpoints and trying to persuade the other person to see and accept your opinions and conclusions. Long ago, I decided to refrain from discussion or arguments over facts that I can easily verify. Even if I have just checked something and know the facts it is useless to argue with someone who is convinced that you are in error.

I recently told our seven-year-old grandson about something that I had learned that I found astonishing. He said, "That can't be true Grandpa." I said, "Justin, if I tell a joke or a funny story I will never claim that it's true if it's not." He looked at me and said "Grandpa, I know you think that what you said is true. I'm just not sure it's accurate." The whole family broke up with laughter.

Consider a recent discussion over whether there is a Social Security Trust fund. Isn't that a "fact" that can be easily verified? It seems so. But the problem is definitional. Two equally informed intelligent people can argue forever about whether there is a Social Security Trust Fund.

A trust fund is a legal arrangement, with a trustee who is responsible for managing, investing, and distributing funds in accordance with the instructions set forth in the trust documents. There is no such "trust fund" for Social Security. Social Security taxes are a part of the general revenue of the U.S. Government. Receipts that are not required to meet current Social Security payments are not handed over to a trustee for investment and management. If the Social Security taxes were set aside in a separate fund, managed and invested, and used solely for the purpose of paying Social Security Benefits, the federal budget deficit would be simply shocking. Until collected funds are needed to make current payments they are "invested" in government bonds. The government loans money to itself. So the argument over whether there is a "Trust Fund" in the usual sense can go on ad infinitum, ad nauseam, and no one will win or lose the argument.

Now let's deal with an issue that's not a definitional problem and not a verifiable fact, but strictly a matter of opinion.

Discussions and Arguments

Frank: "Estate Taxes are the greatest rip-off known to man. You've earned the money, you've paid taxes on it once and carefully saved and invested. Then you die and the government takes 55% of your estate. It's criminal."

Bill: "It's a good way of raising money. It only hits the Fat Cats! Share the wealth."

Frank: "You damn liberals are all alike! Tax and spend. It's my damn money. Why the hell should the government be ripping off my kids after I've worked like a dog to build an estate?"

Bill: "You right wingers never get the point. You were able to make that fortune because you live in this great country, but you never want to pay to support our schools. Let the kids make it on their own. You'll just spoil them if you give them a lot of money."

The Estate Taxes issue is current and significant. It needs to be discussed on its merits, the problems that it creates, its advantages and disadvantages, and the consequences of either amending the law in significant ways or repealing it. It is unlikely that Frank and Bill are going to get to the merits of the issue after they have so emphatically taken a philosophical position and insulted each other in the first few words of their discussion.

After Frank grandly pronounces that "Estate Taxes are the greatest rip-off known to man!" suppose Bill decides that he will disagree without being disagreeable and will try to find some common ground for discussion.

Bill: "Estate taxes are a problem. I understand that some families have to sell their businesses or farms to pay the taxes."

Frank: "Exactly, I'm glad you agree with me."

Bill: "As I understand the present law, the first $675,000 of an estate is not taxed, so a couple can leave their kids over

$1,350,000. That's a pretty tidy sum. And I understand the exempted amount is going up every year."

Frank: "But if I've worked and saved three million bucks, why shouldn't my kids get it? Why the hell should the government get it rather than my kids? I earned the dam money and I managed it."

Bill: "It's a problem. But I understand you can leave the excess funds to charity and avoid the taxes. And with the Social Security problems that the country is facing, if estate taxes are abolished, where will we get the money to pay the federal debt. It seems to me that estate taxes are a better method of raising money than income taxes. Estate taxes affect only your kids, but income taxes reduce the amount that you have available while you are alive."

Frank: "You liberals are all alike. You never saw a tax you didn't like."

Bill: "Actually I hate the income taxes and the employment taxes. That's money I had rather use right now. I hope I can earn enough that I have to pay estate taxes, because that means I will live well, will be able to leave $1,350,000 to the kids, and some money to charity. The law needs to be changed so that families do not lose their farm, which has increased in value because of inflation, and so that people do not lose their family businesses. But, I don't feel too badly if the children of billionaires don't receive an extra half billion dollars. They'll probably get along with only half a billion. Remember what Warren Buffett, one of the richest men in the world says, 'I'll leave enough money to my kids so that they will be able to do something, but not enough that they will be able to do nothing.' That sounds like sound wisdom to me."

Bill has not insulted Frank. He has agreed that the problem is serious, that changes need to be made, that if the taxes are merely repealed the revenue will have to be made up with other taxes that might be even worse and that it is primarily a problem for the super rich.

What Bill has done is address the merits of the issue, has refrained from making provocative remarks, has raised points that Frank may not have considered. Bill has demonstrated respect for Frank's opinion, gained respect for himself, and probably diffused the emotion and hostility. Bill has respectfully invited Frank to engage in a reasonable dialogue and has left the conversation without rancor. While Frank will probably never change his mind, it is possible that, with this approach, he may at least consider the points made by Bill and moderate his stance.

And even if Frank remains with his feet in concrete, with an absolute commitment to repealing that "criminal" tax, he will feel good about Bill and respect him for his civility and willingness to consider another point of view. Consider how much better both will feel about the encounter and about each other as compared to the earlier scenario.

When confronted with a firmly held opinion with which you disagree, one that is pronounced with bombast, take a deep breath, focus on the merits of the issue, refrain from personal remarks and provocative comments, raise points or issues that the other person seems not to have considered, if there is any area of agreement, acknowledge it and then disagree by addressing the merits without being disagreeable. And if you can inject some humor into the discussion it will further diffuse the situation and increase the possibility that the other person will find something in your comments that they can agree with.

If your only relationship with Frank is to play tennis with him twice a week and you have long since realized that he is an opinionated jerk, convinced that he knows everything, is the master of the grand pronouncement, and is not about to enter into civil discourse, much less ever change his mind about anything, then the only thing to do is change the subject.

You might try teasing him a little with the story of the monk who showed up in Heaven. St. Peter warmly greeted him, thanked him for his devotion to helping the poor and disabled, sacrificing all earthly pleasures and living by his vow of poverty. St. Peter showed him to his little shack that was worse than the quarters he just left on earth. The monk looked up and saw this fabulous palace glowing with heavenly light. "Is that God's home?" he asked. "No," answered St. Peter. "That's Warren Buffett's heavenly home." Isn't he the billionaire? Wasn't he one of the richest people on earth?" asked the monk. "Yes, that's him," said St. Peter. "I didn't realize that the wealthy would be able to buy the best places in Heaven while the poor have to live in primitive conditions because they can't afford anything better," reflected the monk. "Oh no," exclaimed St. Peter. "That's not it at all. Heaven is full of monks, but no billionaire has ever made it to Heaven before. We thought we better do something special for this one."

You can finish off the conversation about estate taxes with a smile and an observation, "Maybe billionaires will have a better chance of getting to Heaven if the government takes their money!"

A Dose Of Reality

We know that focusing on the merits of an issue, avoiding provocative comments and trying to engage in civil discourse does not work with Mr. Opinionated. He has his opinions, is comfortable with them, and will probably take them to his grave!

There are also very intelligent individuals with whom you can have civil discourse on controversial issues and agree to disagree without rancor unless they have a financial or emotional involvement in the issue. If a financial issue or a cause is at stake, the merits of the issue become irrelevant and loyalty becomes the issue.

I have a good friend, not a close friend, but a good friend, of longstanding. She has an emotional commitment to a local project. She believes that it is the defining moment for the community. She feels that it should be the number one community priority. It is the compelling force in her life. There are those, including me, who feel that there are problems with the project and that there are more compelling issues facing the community.

I wrote a commentary that was published in the local paper. I carefully laid out verified facts, raised questions about the financial feasibility of the project and questioned whether the project should preempt the commitment of resources to and financing of other community projects. I received a letter from my "friend." She attacked me for disloyalty to the "cause" and suggested that I was a liar. Yet she failed to identify any factual inaccuracies in my piece.

I tried to explain my concern about the project's practical and financial problems and its interference with another important community project. I offered to meet with her and discuss the issues. Her response was, "Charlie, you need to support us and quit lying about this project."

I can give numerous examples of situations where otherwise reasonable individuals, who have personal, financial or emotional involvement in an issue, become alienated if a friend takes a principled, well thought out, and well reasoned position that is in conflict with the original person's position.

The lesson is simple and compelling. Do not assume that the merits of an issue are more important and outweigh the personal feelings of those who have a vested emotional or financial interest in a project.

You effectively listen to a friend. You fundamentally disagree with his or her position. The issue is important to you. Your friend has a vested interest in the outcome of the project. The decision that you face? Is my friendship more important than the issue? No matter how strongly you feel about the merits of the project, you have to realize that if you take a stand in support of your position, you might lose a friend!

This is a situation where attitude affects perception and feelings. We are frequently faced with situations where attitudes affect perceptions and determine feelings.

I often tell the story about the reporter from the San Francisco Chronicle who was at Golden Gate Park in San Francisco enjoying a moment of idleness and watching a couple of young men toss a football. Suddenly a huge dog, with teeth bared, charged one of the men. His companion grabbed a stick, hit the dog, knocked him down, and in the throes of his reaction, shoved the stick under the dog's collar, gave it a violent twist, and suffocated the dog.

The reporter grabbed his ever-present notebook and interviewed the hero. He wrote in his notebook: "San Francisco Forty-Niner fan risks his life to save a friend. He subdues a vicious mad-dog which was on the verge of killing his friend. It was a courageous and death defying act."

The hero observes what the reporter is writing and comments, "I don't like the Forty-Niners. I'm a Dallas Cowboys fan!"

The reporter marks through his earlier notes and writes, "Drunk Texan viciously attacks and kills a family's pet dog in Golden Gate Park while the dog was playfully chasing balls!"

Oh yes, attitudes do affect perceptions and your ability to listen!

Chapter 6

HANDLING PROBLEM PERSONALITIES

Visionary Stephen Wright observes: "No one is listening until you make a mistake." This observation is especially apt to listening that occurs (or does not occur) in meetings and groups.

Dave Barry says, "When trouble arises and things look bad, there is always one individual who perceives a solution and is willing to take command. Very often, that person is crazy." Barry also says, "If you had to identify, in one word, the reason why the human race has not achieved, and never will achieve, its full potential, that word would be "meetings."

One of Murphy's Laws: "Never delay the ending of a meeting or the beginning of a cocktail hour."

On a more serious note, Horace Mann, the great educator, observed, "False conclusions which have been reasoned out are infinitely worse than blind impulse." My sense of this insightful comment is that those "conclusions which have been reasoned out" will be defended to the last breath, while those who blurt out blind impulses will recognize them as such and may be willing to listen to reason.

Problem Personalities In Groups And Meetings

I served on boards of directors of private businesses, non-profit organizations, and government agencies, both elective and appointive, and committees for every conceivable purpose. In short, too many boards and committees for one lifetime. Be assured that you will find one or more of the following "Problem Personalities" on many boards and committees. (For readability I will use the male gender, but that does not mean that these are gender specific problems.)

The Sharer. Every comment reminds him of an incident involving himself and acquaintances. He can't resist sharing the anecdote with you. The anecdote has nothing to do with the issue being discussed and is seldom either interesting or funny.

This is difficult because he is usually well intentioned and pleasant, but chatty. I had one on a board of which I was Chair. I became alert to his body language and learned to anticipate when he was reminded of an anecdote that he wanted to share. I would interrupt him when it was obvious that he was laying the groundwork for an anecdote and say, "Joe, let's just finish up with this problem. During the break you can share that with us." I had built enough trust that he would usually agree to postpone his story.

Mr. Opinion and Conclusion. (Mr. O&C) He has done everything. There is no situation that he has not experienced. The minute the issue or problem is stated he pounces with his opinion and conclusion. He does not want to waste time on the Facts, Analysis, Alternatives, and Consequences of any decision. His opinion and conclusions are carved in stone (in his stone head!). Unfortunately many of these types are bright and articulate and can intimidate other board members, thereby inhibiting constructive discussion.

The way I handle these individuals is, "Larry, that may be a good idea and a good approach, but there are those of us who need a few more facts and some analysis before we make a decision." I then try to frame the issues and identify what facts we are missing. I then suggest that while Larry has an idea of how to deal with this problem, let's look at some other alternatives and discuss how they might work. Listing Larry's suggestion as one of the alternatives lets Larry know that his "solution" will be considered. In addition, as the discussion proceeds and the participants become aware of all of the facts, analyses, and possible consequences of each alternative, the fallacies in Larry's "solution" often become evident to all without having told Larry that it is unworkable and starting an argument.

Mr. Ramrod. Ramrod is similar to Mr. O&C in that he does not want to waste time with the Facts, Analysis, Alternatives, Consequences, and a lot of discussion. Ramrod does not have an opinion or conclusion, he is just too busy to waste time on "trivial" matters. He wants to make a decision and move on to more important matters (possibly his golf game.). His mantra: "Let's just make a decision and move on." He is convinced that he is being efficient and saving everybody's valuable time. When Ramrod prevails, rams through a decision without adequate facts and analysis, and things go wrong, he will not recall his conduct. He will look around for someone to blame.

Don't argue with Ramrod! Try this. "Ram, I know you're on a tight schedule. I appreciate your taking the time to join us. We'll try to get through this efficiently, but there are some facts that need to be brought out and discussed and we will need to consider the consequences of our decision. I will take notes, and if you have to leave before we're finished I will brief you on what we decide and our reasoning."

If Ram has to make the final decision the scenario will

have to be changed. In that case suggest that the group come up with a recommendation and an outline of the reasons and the adverse consequences that might result from other action plans, and that Ram will be given a memorandum soon after the meeting is finished for his review and approval.

Mr. Distraction. Mr. Distraction has too many things on his mind and never plugs in to the discussion. Suddenly he realizes that the group is moving towards a decision and he starts asking questions about matters that have been exhaustively discussed while he was physically present but in another world.

The technique for dealing with him will depend upon his role in the process, Big Boss, Key Player, or Flunky. If he is Big Boss and has too many things on his mind and did not focus on what was happening at the meeting, you might try the following when he finally plugs in and realizes that decisions are being made and he hasn't been listening and is not involved: "Boss, you probably remember that we worked through facts 1, 2, 3, and 4 and concluded that unless we chose alternative 3 rather than 1, 2 or 4, we'll just create further problems such as yada, yada, yada! We sensed that you felt the same way. If you have any other reactions let us know. Otherwise, we are ready to go with the project. This provides an instant briefing, without dwelling on the fact that he was not paying attention. It also gives him the opportunity to buy into the project or express his concerns or disapproval, without making a fool of himself.

If the person is a key player the scenario and technique is pretty much the same. You need to bring him on board, without putting him down, summarize the issues, the facts, the advantages and disadvantages of each alternative, and what seems to be a consensus that everyone felt he seemed to feel comfortable with. This gives him an opportunity to clarify, and express his concerns and suggestions.

If it is Mr. Flunky, who is probably never plugged in, it is wise to be kind and, without putting him down, summarize where you are. This will avoid embarrassment and give everyone a summary of what has been decided and why.

The Charming Schmoozer. He can divert discussion, come up with a hundred general examples of similar problems and solutions, confuse everyone, and cause everyone to wonder whether there really is a problem. If the Schmoozer gets loose, he produces frustration and usually causes a postponement of any decision until the matter can be "clarified."

He will never quit schmoozing, making asides, and moving from the specific to the general. Someone has to take control and say, "Thanks Schmooz. Sharing your experience with us was helpful. We need to get back to our specific problem. Unless we make a decision we may lose our funding for this project. The staff needs to know whether they can hire personnel and get underway. As I see it, here is the issue, the alternatives, and the consequences that we face with each choice. I would like to go around the table and get a reaction. Do we need additional facts or are you ready to make a decision?

Without personally attacking him it brings everyone "home" to the specific problem and kindly exposes Schmooz as someone who has lots of experience which he is willing to share, but is incapable of dealing with specifics.

Mr. Negative. His mantra is: "That'll never work." He has a problem for every solution. He scoffs at anyone who proposes a solution and either implies or states that those who support the proposal are either naïve or ignorant or both.

Nothing is ever going to satisfy Neg. You might try, "Neg, you have brought up important points that we need to consider. We do have to make a decision. There were some suggestions that appear to be workable. I would like to go around the table and get reactions to the proposals made by Mary, Frank, and Joe. Let's stick with the advantages and disadvantages of each of their proposals and see if there are some common elements that we can bring together to address this problem. We all realize that there will never be a perfect solution. But for the rest of the meeting let's stay away from focusing on the 'Parade of Horrible Consequences' that might result from any decision we might make. Let's spend our time focusing on the constructive suggestions that have been offered, distill the best from each, and make a decision."

The Attack Dog. His mantra is: "They are the problem." Dog always operates from the standpoint that "they" screwed it up and no matter what we do "they" will screw it up again. "They" are lazy, ignorant, typical bureaucrats, have an employee mentality, clock-watchers, just putting in their time, a bunch of liberals, or a bunch of right wingers, never get it right, and don't care. So no matter what we do or decide, Dog will just say that it's a waste of time as long as "they" are either in charge, or are the ones carrying out the decision.

When Dog starts attacking the "theys," a polite but firm intervention is necessary. Try something like this. "Dog we do have problems with some of our people. We need to take this into account in dealing with this issue. But first, let's try to put together a workable plan. Let's make sure we have all of the facts, have identified the issue or problem, and get some discussion on a plan of action. We can then address the personnel problems."

This shifts the focus back to the issue or problem and converts the "they" to a personnel problem which is a separate agenda item. Dog will never be satisfied and will try to keep bringing up the "they" issue. But by treating him with dignity and acknowledging that this is an issue that needs attention, it might enable you to move on with the discussion and the problem solving. The last thing that you will want to do is confront him and argue over whether "they" are really the problem.

Mr. Gloomy. That's the way life is. We're going to have to live with this problem. It'll never change. That's just the way life is. He is less aggressive than Mr. Negative but he too can put a pall on any constructive approach to solving a problem.

Mr. Gloomy is not a happy person. But he may garner sympathy from a few participants because they feel sorry for him. So nothing is accomplished by indulging the impulse to say. "Well, Gloomy, shall we all go home, go to bed, pull the sheets over our heads, and just give up?" This or any similar response may stimulate a counter attack or a defense of poor Gloomy. A better approach might be, "Yes, life is a bitch and then you die, but let's see if we can't change life. I have some thoughts about how to deal with this problem and I'm sure others do too. Let's get some ideas and see if we can't solve this, or if not solve it at least improve the situation." Now would be an ideal time to call on Mr. Synthesizer if you have one present. If not, you might want to float your suggestions and solicit reactions.

Mr. Trust Me! "Look, just leave this to me. I have handled problems just like this dozens of times. Let's not make a big deal out of it. Don't worry, be happy, trust me I will get it done." When asked how and when, Mr. Trust Me becomes defensive and a little angry. I told you that I know how to handle this, I've been here a lot longer than you, I know how things work. Don't you worry about it. I'll get it done and in good time.

Mr. Trust Me is a challenge, especially if he is in a position of authority. He's capable of grabbing the ball and running down the field – the wrong way! The key is to find a way to encourage him to think out loud with the group about how he intends to "handle" the problem. One approach might be: "Trust, we're sure that you'll do a good job, but it would be helpful to us if you would share what you have in mind so that we will all know what is happening and can cooperate. I have a feeling that some of the group have ideas that would be helpful. Please briefly outline what you have in mind and let's see if anyone has something helpful to add." If you suggest that, "Let's get everyone's reactions," Trust will again perceive it as a challenge, an expression of doubt about whether he has the problem in hand. The point is to get Trust to understand and believe that it is important to have everyone understand what is happening and to be on the same playing field.

The Sniper (The Whisperer). He repeatedly leans over to the individuals sitting on each side of him and whispers a constant stream of snide remarks putting down everything that is said and every speaker. He's a basher. He's never heard any comment that makes sense. He never participates in the discussion, confining his put-downs and snide remarks to his immediate neighbors. His mantra is: "Oh my God, can you believe what he just said! That's so ridiculous!"

Every Sniper shares the common compulsion to impose on his neighbors and ridicule what everyone is saying. He thinks that he is enhancing his own image by demonstrating that he recognizes everyone's stupidity and that he and possibly his neighbors are the only ones in on the farce that is taking place. But, while sharing the same compulsion each Sniper will have a different personality. The technique for dealing with them will have to be adapted to their individual quirks. However, making the Sniper aware that everyone else is aware of him and his distracting and disruptive conduct, if done in a non-confrontational way, can temporarily put a stop to the conduct. One approach might be to say, "Snipe, it seems as if you have some thoughts and reactions to what Jane just said. Please share them. We all want to know what you're thinking, not just those sitting next to you." This will usually inhibit Snipe from continuing his whispering. When he is singled out in this way, he may wait and do his sniping after the meeting.

Mr. Isn't It Wonderful. No matter what happens, even if nothing is accomplished, his response is "Wasn't that a wonderful meeting. What a good team. We were really communicating. I'm looking forward to our next meeting. This is such fun." He might be called Mr. Clueless. Hearing his comments, you probably wonder whether you were even at the same meeting. The one that you sat through went nowhere.

Depending on how concise and articulate Mr. Wonderful is, one technique for bringing him on board and possibly teaching him how to be a more effective participant is to suggest: "Wonderful, why don't you check your notes and summarize for us what we have agreed to do and outline our plan of action." This might accomplish two things. It suggests that had he taken notes he would be aware of what was happening and that he better plug into the meeting because he might be called on to summarize what the meeting is about and what it accomplished.

Mr. Let's You Do It. Mr. Let's routine runs something like this: "Hey, our sales are in the tank! We've got to get this solved. I don't want to waste a lot of time kicking this around. Joe, you're the sales manager, so I want you to get out front on this problem. Find out what's wrong and get it done. I want those sales up. I want a full report in 10 days and it better be positive." When Joe tries to explain that the reason sales are down is a combination of the factory being unable to get product out and that many of the widgets they were shipping are defective, Mr. Let's' response is: "I didn't ask for excuses. I want you to solve the problem." Of course Joe has nothing to do with production. But Mr. Let's ain't about to listen.

It's never going to work for Joe to suggest a solution or a different approach. Mr. Let's will perceive any suggestion by Joe, the target, as an excuse. Someone other than Joe might suggest: "There may be some production problems affecting sales. Let me get together with Joe and the Production Manager, get the facts, check with some of our customers, look at what the competition is doing, get an outline of the problem, some suggestions for dealing with it, and be ready to "DISCUSS" some possible approaches at our meeting in 10 days." This enables the speaker to serve as a foil and a shield for Joe and convert the approach from "having the problem solved" in 10 days to defining the problem and seeking realistic solutions and promoting a cooperative effort.

Mr. Let's Have a Meeting. Meeting thinks that having a meeting is the best – maybe the only – way to solve a problem. He has yet to learn that a meeting will be a waste of time unless the problem is defined, the facts gathered, some analysis done, and alternatives considered along with possible consequences. With this preparation in hand, a meeting can be fruitful, shed light on the cause of the problem, and identify the consequences of any course of corrective action. When he holds a meeting without preparation and nothing is accomplished, he blames the participants and concludes the meeting with, "We better meet again next week. We've got to solve this problem."

Suggesting to Meeting that it is useless, an exercise in futility to meet without a purpose, without an agenda, and without preparation, will merely provoke an argument and waste time. A response that might work is: "That sounds like a good idea. I'll get together with appropriate members of the staff, prepare an agenda, circulate a memorandum with the Facts, Analysis, Alternatives, and Consequences, and set a meeting date far enough in advance to enable everyone to digest the memo. Help me out. I want to be sure what topic or issue you want to deal with at the meeting." This is an offer to cooperate. It will expose, in a non-insulting way, that if there is not a problem or issue that needs to be dealt with, no meeting is necessary.

We Can't Make a Decision! We Haven't Considered all of the Alternatives. No Decision will never be willing to vote for a solution because there must be alternatives that have not been considered and therefore we "might be making a mistake!" The possibility of making a mistake disables No Decision.

Since alternatives are always infinite, No Decision will never be able to make a decision. The problem is enabling him to deal with reality without challenging his perfectly valid concern that there are always other alternatives. Suggesting that he will never be satisfied or that he will always find a reason for not making a decision will simply stimulate his imagination, and his propensity to march out the "Parade of Horribles!" He will go through all of the horrible things that might happen if we fail to consider all of the alternatives. It is necessary to find a way to relieve his pain. If he is a key player, you might suggest that it is necessary to deal with the problem immediately. The proposed plan, while not perfect, enables you to start dealing with the problem. You can then add, "But, you're right, there are probably other alternatives. Let's start dealing with the problem. Meanwhile we will explore the other alternatives and modify the plan as we go."

Mr. I, My, Me. IMyMe is a composite of many of the individuals described above. He has to be the center of attention. "Let me tell you what I think." "My opinion or feeling is ..." "If you ask me ..." (nobody did!). He interrupts, fills every pause and, if permitted, will dominate the discussion. He is totally insensitive to dramatic pauses which enable participants to assimilate, contemplate, and constructively respond to thoughtful and insightful comments.

In many ways, this may be the most difficult individual to deal with. Any effort to cut him off will provoke him, "Wait a minute. I thought we were here to discuss this problem and get everyone's ideas. Can't I comment or express my views? What's wrong with my ideas? Everyone else has been given a chance to talk. What about me?" IMyMe is unaware that he has dominated the discussion. The best way of dealing with him is: "Why don't you lead off. Then I want to go around the table and get everyone else's reaction. I urge everyone to keep their comments brief and to the point. We're running out of time." This sets the stage for interrupting if he goes on and on. "Thanks IMyMe. I'm sorry to interrupt, but I want to give everyone an opportunity to comment. Let's move on to the next person." IMyMe will want to comment after each speaker. But you have set the stage to say, "Let's listen to Jane, (the next person in line) give her reactions and then we will, if we have time, try to give everyone time to respond after everyone has had a chance to comment."

There ARE individuals who are excellent board or committee members. Let's call them the Synthesizers.

> They listen.
> They try to be sure that the problem is defined so that everyone understands the problem and is dealing with the same issue.

They take notes.

They attempt to clarify and summarize the Facts, Analysis, Alternatives, and Consequences.

They deal with the problem personalities with kindness, humor, and firmness.

They are not patronizing or arrogant. No matter how tempting, they do not put down, embarrass, or criticize participants.

When discussion appears to be complete on an important issue and at the end of the meeting, Synthesizers suggest that it would be helpful to go around the table and ask each participant to give reactions and input. They ask that this be done without interrupting the speaker. As each person finishes, they say something like, "Thank you," then pause and say: "Let me be sure I understand your point." They then play back a summary of what was said. They are skillful enough to vary the wording and the technique to avoid being mechanical and boring.

Encouraging Input from The Quiet Ones

Meetings are frequently dominated by one or more individuals. Often there are individuals present who say nothing because of shyness, being intimidated, or being afraid that what they have to say may sound stupid. These Quiet Ones may have important insights or reactions. This technique is designed to bring out suggestions and reactions from those who are not assertive enough to break into the discussion, but who might have insightful constructive thoughts and proposals to offer.

Asking everyone to comment and react, without being interrupted, is a non-threatening way of having them contribute. The summary, after they have commented, assures them that they have been heard. It gives them the opportunity to clear up any misunderstanding and makes them feel that they are a part of the team.

Summarizing the comments and having the speaker acknowledge that their comments have been understood is very important. It clears up any confusion, demonstrates that you have listened and understood. It forces the speaker to either buy into your understanding or clarify their comments. This process often exposes, in a non-antagonistic, non-confrontational manner, any fallacies in the comments and reactions of the participants.

I have used this approach to good advantage when serving as chair or president of organizations. It has enabled me to draw out worthwhile contributions and insights that would never have emerged if this technique had not been used.

Obtaining Information Without Being Confrontational

When I was Foreman of the Grand Jury working with eighteen other members, I had to develop certain tools for dealing with a remarkable variety of individuals. I found that when the discussion drifted away from the issues, became heated or disjointed, I could most effectively deal with the problem by posing non-confrontational questions.

"How do you suggest that we handle the problem?" forces a person to focus on remedies and be specific rather than engaging in a philosophical discussion or relating anecdotes.

"What would you do if you were in charge, if you were the Czar?" proved to be a very effective question to smoke out ideas from government employees who had a lot of knowledge and experience but found that no one was soliciting their input nor listening to them. This question was also effective in gently squelching and exposing those who had lots of opinions and conclusions but no constructive solutions. This question gave individuals, whether members of the Grand Jury or witnesses, the opportunity to offer solutions if they had any, without a dozen excuses.

"What do you think about this approach; do you see any flaws or problems in approaching it this way?" enabled me to float ideas and proposals without appearing to attempt to control the process. This question was then followed by a carefully thought out approach to the problem that I was pretty sure would work. Compare this to saying, "I'VE GIVEN THIS A LOT OF THOUGHT AND THIS IS WHAT WE SHOULD DO!" The earlier approach usually stimulates constructive discussion and suggestions while the latter is designed to provoke arguments.

Concluding Meetings

At the conclusion of every meeting, if possible and appropriate, Mr. Synthesizer says something like, "For my benefit I'd like to state my understanding of what we have decided, what needs to be done, who is responsible for each task, and the time line. I just want to be sure that I know what I am supposed to do and that I understand what everyone else will be doing. Please bear with me for a minute." After he finishes with his summary he will ask, "Is that consistent with everyone else's understanding of what we decided that we need to do and when we need to do it?"

This technique is a civil request for clarification, confirmation, and ratification of the outcome of the meeting. It also lays the groundwork for offering to share a memo of your summary with the participants. This will put everyone on notice that you have made a record of the outcome. This will further enhance the ratification process.

Listening in Public Meetings

I learned significant lessons about listening in public meetings from a very good friend, Gerald "Jerry" Fry. I was on the Monterey City Council at the time, and he was the Mayor. We were on the opposite ends of the political spectrum.

There were many volatile meetings over controversial issues. The Council chambers would fill with angry people, half in favor of a project, half against, each group vehement. Everyone wanted to speak. There was never enough time. Speakers would make points with great passion. The next one would repeat the points with equal passion.

Jerry had a remarkable technique for diffusing the meeting. Before opening the controversial item to public comment, he would acknowledge everyone's desire to be heard. He then summarized, better than the speakers, the points to be made on each side. He would then suggest that, while we would stay as long as necessary, he hoped that speakers would refrain from repeating the same points over and over. He asked for a show of hands of those in favor and in opposition.

Jerry would then briefly summarize the point after each speaker finished, acknowledge that we understood the point, and express hope that other speakers would not merely repeat the points.

His masterful, sympathetic, and witty handling of the situation made the audience aware that they were being heard and that their views would be considered. This diffused the anger, shortened the meeting, and made the audience feel that they were participating in a democratic process.

In "The Other Side of Language," Fiumara observes:

> "A discerning act of listening, therefore, demands a strength and rigor that are difficult to subjugate and that deserve constant exercise. A listening atmosphere is not improvised. It is, on the contrary, the product of a strenuous process of conception, growth and devoted attention."

CHAPTER 7

A GARDEN VARIETY OF LISTENING SITUATIONS

Listening Between The Lines · Separating the Message from the Words

As a lawyer it is essential to listen to your clients, hear what they say, read their body language, watch their eyes, and then frame questions which will bring out all of the facts and background of the matter about which they are consulting you. By taking the jumble of facts presented and defining the issue or the question, and then playing it back to the client, the solution is often obvious. Sometimes, defining the issue demonstrated that there was no problem at all. There were also times when defining the issue demonstrated that there was a problem with no solution. By identifying the lack of a solution we were able to identify steps which needed to be taken to move on.

Listening as a part of practicing law also means "listening through" the words of witnesses, judges, and other lawyers to find the message behind the words, or as the French philosopher Michel Foucault called it: "hearing what was being said in what was said."

I became quite skilled in deposing and cross-examining witnesses. I was always thoroughly prepared and usually knew the facts better than the witness. I knew when they were being inaccurate. I was able to have a number of cases thrown out before trial based on a deposition of a key witness. Other cases against my clients collapsed during trial because of the depositions I had taken or my cross-examination of witnesses during trial. I would not have been able to accomplish this without well-honed listening skills.

How does one tell when the message is different from the words being spoken? Not easily! It can be done but, like most things, it requires identifying and learning the necessary skills and practicing them.

Start with hearing the words and examining the words in your mind while watching the body language, the eyes, and other "evidentiary" conduct and markers. At the simplest level, we all know that the kid who has chocolate all over his mouth is probably lying when he says he did not eat the candy! But most evidence is not that clear and convincing. But the eyes, the hands, and the presence or absence of body tension says a lot. The problem is figuring out what.

It is normal for someone to be tense, anxious, and nervous when having a deposition taken by an opposing lawyer. But I deal with that situation by taking the time to engage the witness, to build trust and credibility, and to make sure the witness is relaxed and comfortable with the process. I build slowly to the critical issues and questions about which the witness might want to be evasive or about which they might have discomfort with a straightforward, honest answer. I then know that the nervousness, tension, shifty eyes, unconscious "wringing of hands," the glance at his or her lawyer for help or guidance, and other messages emerge from wrestling with being accurate rather than with tension, which naturally arises in the threatening circumstance of a deposition.

Carefully composed, but not challenging questions can help work through to the message behind the words in normal, routine, daily relationships with spouses, children, friends, co-workers, and superiors.

Let's say you are carrying on a serious conversation with someone. As you hear the words and watch the eyes, the hands, and the tension of the speaker, something seems amiss. It may be again time for the "help me understand" approach. Sort through anything in the words that does not fit the circumstances as you know them, is inconsistent with the general demeanor of the speaker, or does not fit in with what you know about the speaker.

Frame a non-threatening question, "I understand that you want a Mercedes. Help me understand how you're going to pay for it. I didn't quite follow what you said." This is more likely to enable you to reach a resolution of the issue than, for example, "Are you crazy? We're trying to save money for a down payment on a house and you want to spend a small fortune on a new luxury car. What the hell are you doing?"

> In the August 5, 2002 issue of The New Yorker Magazine, there is a fascinating article by Malcolm Gladwell entitled "The Naked Face: Can you read people's thoughts just by looking at them?" The article deals with the scientific work by a psychologist named Paul Ekman and his collaborator, Wallace Friesen, in studying and creating a taxonomy of facial expressions. It is a very impressive article. It convinced me that with enough study of the research and findings of Ekman, Friesen, and others, and with a disciplined practice, one can read messages that the speaker does not know that s/he is delivering. Gladwell's article deals with some remarkable examples of "face reading" of contemporary public figures, such as Bill Clinton.

If the response is: "It's the end of the model year. They are discounting Mercedes big time with no down payment, 1.9% financing, and no payments for 60 days. And with a Mercedes I'll be able to impress my clients, sell a lot more real estate, and make a lot more money," you have a serious problem. But, by not launching an attack, there may be hope that you can reason through the problem and convince your spouse that when the payments start in 60 days the two of you will be unable to put away funds for the down payment on the home.

There is no one technique for listening through the words and finding the message or the "what was being said in what was said." But, the possibility of drawing out the actual message is greatly improved by framing non-threatening questions, such as: "Help me understand," "Help me through this," "Help me out, I'm having trouble following what you're saying,"

Each effort will depend on the personality of the other person and the credibility of the relationship you have with them, as well as your skills in avoiding confrontational statements or questions. Which brings us to a critical point that must be made: the process of listening, working through the words to the message, and hearing what was being said in what was said, does not involve agreement, consent, approval, or submission.

Voltaire said: "I detest what you say but will defend to the death your right to say it!" If he were writing this book, he might say: "I detest what you say, but I will LISTEN and defend to the death your right to say it."

Listening means hearing and understanding what the speaker is saying and affirming that you heard and understood the message. In affirming that you understand the message, it is important not to communicate, inadvertently, that you agree with the speaker or approve of what s/he said or consent to or submit to the comment, proposal, or suggestion. I can hear you, acknowledge what you say, and affirm that "I got the message," without agreeing with you or consenting to anything. I may disagree with what you say. Even if I disagree, a constructive purpose has been accomplished by the listening.

Trying to Listen When You Are Insecure or Anxious

In a situation where you are insecure or anxious about the listening event, it is difficult to listen effectively. You may

A Garden Variety of Listening Situations

be thinking about what the other person or persons are thinking about you. You may be afraid of sounding stupid, or you may be intimidated by the company or the circumstances, as in a job interview. The Relax &Focus technique is an important technique to use in these situations.

Cross-Cultural Listening

Sometimes listening between the lines is necessary when dealing with cultures that are less direct than ours or that consider certain types of communication to be impolite or even highly inappropriate. You might not know what a particular culture considers to be the right thing to say, but you can learn very quickly by listening. For example, in some countries it is never polite to discuss business or any potentially controversial or adversarial subject matter during a meal. Before you open your mouth and insert your foot, listen to what everyone else is saying and follow their lead.

My son Chris is married to a Persian woman, Farnoosh. One morning I was up early and fixing breakfast, when Chris and Farnoosh stopped by.

"I fixed a bowl of fruit. Would you like some?" I asked.

"No, dad, I don't want to take your fruit," responded Farnoosh.

"Farnoosh, there's plenty of fruit. Do you want some?"

"What about Mom?" she asked, referring to her mother-in-law.

"I already fixed a bowl for her the way she likes it. Don't you want some? It's fresh from the Farmers Market."

"I will wait until everyone finishes. If there's any left I might have some," she offered.

"Farnoosh, do you want some fruit?" I asked, my voice rising with my frustration.

Chris chuckled and I looked at him quizzically.

"Dad, she's 'tahroafing' with you," he explained.

In the Persian culture you can't say: "I would love to have a bowl of fruit." That would be impolite and therefore unacceptable. Instead, a little ritual must be observed. You can't appear too eager or greedy! So even if you are dying for the fruit you must politely lie and do the "Oh no, I couldn't!" routine.

There is another side to "tahroafing." Chris' mother-in-law had a bad day. It was terribly hot, yet she had cleaned house, fixed dinner, and cleaned up. She used her last bit of energy to hand-squeeze a tall glass of orange juice, then dragged herself up the stairs to enjoy the juice and rest. On the way to her room, she noticed Chris sitting on his bed perspiring. She brightened up, smiled, and went to Chris, saying: "I squeezed a glass of orange juice for you Chris." Knowing his mother-in-law and the circumstances, Chris exploded in laughter.

Farnoosh and I have now developed our own ritual. "Don't tahroaf with me Farnoosh, eat the damn fruit I fixed for you," I say with a smile. She loves to catch me up short. She will offer me something or say, "Let me do those dishes, Dad." If I play coy and say, "You don't have to do that Farnoosh." She rolls her eyes, smiles, and says: "Don't tahroaf with me, Dad!"

As with so many cultures, these are deeply embedded patterns of behavior, in this case designed for avoiding direct and candid responses to genuine efforts to share. Unless and until a cultural pattern is understood there can be an awkwardness. Once you understand that these embedded cultural messages produce reflex responses, you can deal with them with humor and understanding.

Listening & Responding To Children

The most important two words in listening and responding to children are BE THERE.

What was that you say? "You can't listen without being there?"

True! But, we are often physically present yet unaware and not listening.

In earlier chapters, we talked about the problems created by a curt response such as, "Not Now!" when someone says, "I need to talk with you about something." We discussed some techniques that would avoid their feeling rejected and resentful if the moment was "impossible" and the matter was not urgent. If such a response is difficult for an adult to handle, just think of its impact on a child.

For example, you are putting the final brushstrokes on a table you're refinishing and can't be interrupted or you are putting a final flourish of icing on a cake for tonight's party. Little Billy comes in from outside.

Billy: "Mommy, Daddy."
Mom & Dad in unison: "Not now, Billy!"

No one can fault you for buying just a few minutes to complete your project. Both of you finally finish your projects. Only a couple of minutes have elapsed.

Mom: "What is it, Billy?"
Billy: "Someone left the gate open and little sister is across the street."

There does not have to be a potential tragedy to create confusion and hurt feelings in a child. He may have seen the first robin of spring. Will the message be, "Robins are not important?" Is it too much to ask, "What is it Billy?" And if it's a robin, "I will be out in just a minute. Don't scare him off."

And even if he is a typical child and says, "No, you have to come right now," a response from you that "I can't come right now but I will be there in just a minute," might satisfy him. Even if this response does not quell his impatience, he at least knows that you heard him and want to share the robin with him. You are now set up to explain to Billy, at a quiet moment, why you could not dash outside when he called you.

Billy might learn three lessons. Everything cannot happen at once. Patience must be learned. There are times when others have important things to do. You cannot be available for him at every instant unless it is an emergency.

If those responsible for a child listen and administer discipline consistently, firmly, and with love, the child will, in my opinion, learn self-discipline, including a disciplined pattern of effective listening.

My experience with four sons and six grandchildren convinces me that one basic technique in dealing with children is critical. From the first few days of a child's life it is important to make eye contact and smile with a friendly loving expression. This small effort will greatly influence and have an enormous positive effect on the child's visage, demeanor, responsiveness, and ability to listen.

None of our grandchildren live in our town. Our time together is once or twice a month except when we gather as a family for holidays and vacations. When we're together, I make it a point to spend as much time as possible in activities that enable us to have eye contact. I read them stories and have them repeat what they've just heard so we share the joy, sorrow, or humor at the moment. This enables us to get better acquainted, reinforces the story in the child's mind, and seems to build good listening skills.

I am constantly amazed at how well the grandchildren know me, notwithstanding the infrequency of our contacts.

We know of course that children learn to do most things by mimicking those with whom they spend most of their time, usually their parents and siblings or extended family.

We know that children learn to speak, develop extensive vocabularies, pick up the structure of the language, and manage how to articulate surprisingly complex ideas and concepts before receiving formal schooling in language. Isn't it probable that they will also mimic our listening patterns as they observe us in our relationships with our spouses and the child's siblings?

Taking the time to stop what you are doing, make eye contact with the child, and acknowledge what the child says will be an important lesson in how to listen, which the child will hopefully mimic.

Once my wife and the four kids were skiing in Yosemite. After a long day we were heading to the cabin. The driver ahead of me was driving 20 miles an hour when 40 miles per hour was perfectly safe. The driver did not use the turnouts on the two lane winding road. After what seemed like an eternity (probably 10 minutes) there was a straightaway. I passed screaming, "You stupid idiot." Needless to say the younger

---

A new house was bring built on a vacant lot next door. It was summer and eight year old Linda was bored. She asked her parents if she could go over and watch the building of the new house. With strict instructions about not getting in the way or bothering the crew they said yes.

Linda met the crew when they arrived on Monday morning and spent the day watching them. When she saw that they brought their lunches and ate at the site, she brought her lunch the next day and ate with the crew.

Not one to just sit around, Linda made herself useful. She fetched tools, swept up dropped nails, and helped the crew clean up the site at the end of each day. At quitting time on Friday, the foreman called Linda over. "You have been very helpful. Here are your wages," he said, handing her a crisp $10 bill.

Linda ran home to tell her parents. Her father was so impressed that he took Linda to the bank to open up an account for her. The banker was a family friend, and Linda's father proudly told him the story of his hard-working daughter's first week on the job.

With a tear in his eye, the banker praised Linda and then asked, "Are you going back to work next week?"

Linda smiled "Yes, that is if those damned s—theads at the lumber yard get off their lazy asses and deliver the f—ing sheet rock on Monday!"

two assumed that this was what you said when you passed a car, and did so. They had trouble understanding why I could do it and not them. A painful lesson in how children learn bad conduct from listening to and mimicking parents.

Listening to Children Who Are Not Family Members.

There are times when we are with children, sometimes involuntarily, with whom we have no relationship, about whom we know nothing, and so do not know what to expect by way of behavior. This can be in social settings when friends or acquaintances bring their children, or it can be in parks, public places, or on trains or planes.

Obviously the age of the child will be the controlling factor in how you approach, deal with, listen to, and respond to the child. But as mentioned above, most children, regardless of age, respond to eye contact, smiles, attention, and genuine interest in their activities and what they have to say.

Standing in lines at grocery stores, drug stores, banks, and airlines, I seem to be able to stimulate a smile or a giggle from children of all ages with eye contact, a smile and, if appropriate, a question that gives them a chance to get involved.

As in all other listening events, relaxing and focusing is essential. Affirmation usually occurs when you playback what the child has said. Questions that offer the child an opportunity to talk about his or her activities or interests are usually effective in establishing a constructive and positive contact with the child, especially when you listen and demonstrate, through some of the techniques outlined in this book, that you heard what was said. Such efforts do not have to involve significant time commitments. A listening event with a child can be accomplished in a few moments of relaxed and focused attention.

The Dating Scene

Not every "interview" is a formal structured situation such as a job interview. But we are constantly trying to obtain information from and about others in order to make decisions. For example: Is this the person I want to be my doctor, my stockbroker, my investment advisor, my real estate broker, my editor, my electrician, plumber, gardener etc., or is this the person I want as a friend or a spouse.

My wife of 50 years died about two years ago. I wanted a companion with whom to share my life. What more important "interview" could there be than one designed to determine whether you have found your Mr. or Ms. Right? Of course we do not refer to these situations as interviews! We call it "dating." But, while the "date" may be appear to be just an enjoyable occasion, dinner, dancing, or the theater, if you are the least bit serious about living together or getting married, then you are constantly interviewing in an attempt to determine whether this is the right person for you, whether you will be compatible and able to enjoy each other's company through the stresses, strains, and joys of life.

In doing such an important interview you must listen very carefully, skillfully frame and pose questions, and raise issues that will reveal to you the way the other person will react and respond to inevitable disappointments, illness, financial strains, stresses of travel, family conflicts, and the myriad events that make up life.

Here again it is critical to hear what is being said in what is said. For example, critical comments about other relationships, about children; what someone "cannot stand;" comments or conduct that are inappropriate or insensitive in a particular situation or in certain company; descriptions of what they find upsetting; sources of anger or bitterness; what one finds emotionally satisfying, touching, or moving; response to humor, the ability to laugh at oneself in awkward situations; all of these provide critical insights into another person. But in order to gain these important insights you must listen effectively.

Listening and Responding To Questions

There are many barriers to answering questions directly: anxiety, fear, guilt, unwillingness to make a commitment, inability to choose between alternatives, and probably many other concerns as well. The problem is worrying about "why" someone is asking the question. "What do they really mean?" and "What are they getting at?" That worry, conscious or unconscious, interferes with listening to and focusing on the question and being able to give a direct answer.

Recently a former partner and his wife, good friends, dropped by. As they were walking out the door, I mentioned that I was writing a book on listening. He smiled, looked at my wife with a twinkle in his eye, and asked: "Is Charlie a good listener?"

My wife responded, "Well, considering that we've been married almost 48 years, we get along pretty well. But like other couples we have our misunderstandings." Our friends were late for another gathering and moved on without further conversation about my book.

With trepidation, and with all the delicacy I could muster, I said, "I don't believe you answered Phil's question."

"Well," she said, "I wasn't sure what he was asking."

With increasing misgivings, I asked, "Do you remember the question?"

She thought for a moment and said, "I think he asked if you were a good listener. I don't think I answered that. I thought he was asking something else. I didn't really handle that very well. Maybe I need to read your book."

When You Don't Have All The Answers

One of the most difficult lessons that I had to learn about listening to and responding to questions was to say with comfort, "I don't know." I'll not try to sort out the psychology of my problem. But when I finally was able to say, comfortably, "I don't know," my life became a little easier and my relationships with others became more comfortable.

If it is something that I should know, I respond, "I don't know but I will look it up and find the answer." Other times I admit that I don't know the answer to the specific question but do know something about the situation. I offer to share that knowledge if the other person wants to continue the discussion accepting my limited knowledge. This approach avoids that which often happens, answering a different question than was asked. That is diverting and often frustrating.

Suppose a business partner suggests that the company computer has excess capacity. He feels that "we" should hire a couple of people who could handle billing and accounting for other local businesses and increase revenue. He asks, "What do you think?" If your reaction is: "It won't work!" you need to work out a response, without saying, "That's the most stupid idea I've ever heard, it stinks!"

One approach that might preserve a good relationship, "Joe, I'm not sure that it'll work. Let me think about it. If you have worked up some figures and an analysis why don't you share them with me. I'll go over them, give it some thought."

Is this a "direct" response to the question? While it does not communicate your gut reaction, it is "direct" in that it acknowledges the idea, responds to the issue, and sets up a process for a more definitive response.

Suppose Joe presses you for an immediate categorical response because he has a couple of people he wants to hire.

He is concerned that they may not be available if there's a delay. It's probably time to be a little more candid and direct so that the train does not leave the station. Try, "Joe, I want you to know that I'm not comfortable with the proposal. I don't want to move ahead until I have a few more facts and have an opportunity to think about it. I'll get back to you tomorrow (or in a few days). But, in the meantime, please put the idea on hold and don't make any commitments."

Joe now knows that you have listened, you understand his idea, and you are willing to consider it. But, you don't think it will work. You have also made it very clear that you don't want any commitments made to the project until you have had time to analyze it and think about it.

If the proposal comes from your boss rather than your partner, your response will have to be modified to fit the relationship. You might try, "Interesting idea boss. Can I have time think about it? I'm sure you've done an analysis. If I can review the analysis and your cost and revenue estimates I'll be in a better position to evaluate the proposal and give you my thoughts and reactions."

This response buys time, shows that you are willing to help in making sure the project is workable and, if the boss has not done an analysis, points out this significant failure in a non-provocative way.

If the boss says, "I don't have time to go through a lot of analysis. I want to get better utilization of that expensive computer," this is a challenge that requires tact and skill in expressing your concern, without appearing to be negative or critical. Try, " Boss, you asked for my reaction. I do have some concerns. Could we just hold off for a few days before making any commitments? I will give it serious thought and analysis. Why don't we set a time next week that I can sit down and discuss it with you. That will give me time to work up some figures and think through my concerns."

This approach lets the boss know, in a non-challenging

A Garden Variety of Listening Situations

way, that there are issues that need to be considered, that you will work on the project, but that an immediate decision is not a good idea.

Then there are those moments where you are confronted with a question with less serious consequences.

Wife: "Where did you get the strawberries, dear?"
Husband: "They're the first of the season. They may not be that good."
Wife: "Where did you get them?"
Husband: "They were pretty expensive. I hope they're good."
Wife: "Where did you buy them?"
Husband: "Why don't you just try them."
Wife: "I'd really like to know where you bought them so I can get some for my party tomorrow."

Husband is so defensive he doesn't hear the question. In fact he refuses to hear the question. The result? Both parties have become frustrated and irritated. It's going to be a long evening.

Compare this scenario.

Wife: "Where did you get the strawberries?"
Husband: "At Safeway. They were expensive and since they're the first of the season they may not be the greatest. I hope you enjoy them."
Wife: "Thank you. You know how much I love strawberries. That was very thoughtful. I'll go to Safeway and get some for my party tomorrow. I'm so glad you found them."

It'll be a better evening.

There is an old male chauvinist story: Ask a man where he got the can of beans and he answers: "Albertson's." Ask a woman where she got the can of beans and she'll say: "What's wrong with the can of beans?" The inability to or unwillingness to answer questions directly has no single cause or explanation, and is certainly not a gender related problem.

There will often be times when the question needs to be clarified and when a simple yes or no answer either will not work or will be provocative or possibly misleading. But once the question is understood, and a direct but non-provocative answer is framed and delivered you will find that:

>Frustrations are reduced.
>There is less chance of provoking irritation.
>Communication is improved.
>Your relationship with the other person is improved.
>It's easier to deal with the issue at hand.
>Tension will be reduced – and tension is an exhausting waste of energy.

Communicating with Doctors, Lawyers, And Accountants

As a lawyer I learned a lot from my clients, while hopefully helping them solve problems. One client for whom I handled many complicated transactions was a master at managing our professional relationship. He organized all of the materials that I needed to handle a transaction. He prepared a summary of the problems, the questions he wanted answered or the product he wanted me to produce, such as a contract, estate plan, etc. He would deliver these materials to my secretary and set an appointment far enough in advance to enable me to review the materials, do the necessary research, and develop a plan of action. He would then call my secretary to inquire whether I had read the materials and prepared for our meeting, and whether I needed more information or time. (Note, at this point he has not incurred legal fees by talking to me, but he is getting the message through: Charlie, Be Prepared!)

When he arrived for the appointment, he would suggest

that I make any phone calls that were pressing and do anything that might distract me during our meeting. Once I had committed to him that I was ready and that we would not be interrupted, he would tell me what a wonderful lawyer I was and how much I had helped him and his family. By this time I was charged up and ready to totally devote myself to his projects. We had very productive sessions, efficient and cost effective. I realize that I did some of my very best work for him.

If you are going to meet with a lawyer or an accountant call the office and ask if you can pick up a checklist of the information and materials that you will need and the questions which you will be expected to answer. Assemble all such documents and materials, organize them in folders or envelopes, and prepare a summary of the materials and the questions that you need answered.

Deliver the materials and the summary of issues and questions a few days in advance of the appointment and ask that the secretary remind the lawyer or accountant to review them and to call in advance of the meeting if additional information will be needed.

This process should avoid the need for multiple meetings before the project can get under way. Since lawyers and accountants charge for their time, you can reduce the cost of the services and improve the quality of the end product if you do your homework. But you can only do effective homework if you know in advance what information will be needed to handle the problem.

With doctors the situation is a little different because you cannot always anticipate when medical services will be needed. But you can be sure that at some point you will need medical care. When that time comes, prepare a summary of your medical history, including dates if possible. Identify any allergies, any medicines to which you are allergic, family medical history (at very least that of your mother, father, and siblings). List any medicines that you are taking, including any non-prescription medicines that you frequently take. List the reason for taking the medicines, whether it is a matter of recurring heartburn or something more serious.

If you have the time and opportunity, before meeting with the doctor, prepare a detailed description of the symptoms and the questions you want answered. If you can get the summary of your medical history, medicines, and the description of the symptoms and your questions to the doctor in advance of your appointment, you will not only save time, but your appointment will be a more productive one.

Most people get a little nervous in a doctor's office. It is easy to forget something that is important to you. Many doctors seem rushed. This puts additional pressure on the patient to be efficient. This can result in the failure to disclose important information or failure to get answers to questions. If both you and the doctor have in hand a description of the symptoms and the questions you have prepared this problem is less likely to occur

Finally, be prepared to take notes. Write down your understanding of what the doctor says, his answers to your questions, and his recommendations. Then say, I want to be sure I understand. Then read back your understanding of the conversation. That is the time to clear up any misunderstanding or confusion. This will also enable you and the doctor to avoid follow-up phone calls "clarifying" the advice and the course of action which you are to take. It will also give you a record to which you can refer later, in the event that you forget what was said.

These simple tools will enable you to obtain better quality services and advice from your advisors and reduce the cost of their services.

Telling a Good Joke & Anecdote

What do stories and jokes have to do with a book on listening? Ask yourself how often you hear people say, "I wish I could remember jokes!" Actually jokes are in some ways the easiest kinds of stories to remember.

Stories are part of the fabric of our life. They help transmit our culture, values, knowledge, wisdom, judgment, and ethics to our children, friends, and fellow workers. They are a way of sharing experiences and learning about ourselves. From stories we learn that we are not alone in the world or in our feelings. We learn that others share our offbeat thoughts and do offbeat things.

The Bible is a book of stories, about creation, adventure, inspiring feats, interesting, and unique characters, trials, and tribulations. Think of what we would miss without the likes of Tom Sawyer and Huck Finn? Think of the joy that "The Wizard of Oz" brings to us and our children, while we are learning life's lessons about difficult and insecure people, kind and generous people (who have a heart), and at the same time recognizing these feelings within ourselves.

Jokes are short stories that comment on our culture. Surprise and twisted punch lines are what make jokes funny. The reason that people "can never remember jokes" is that they do not listen effectively. They laugh and move on but do not play it back in their head. They do not write down the punch line.

A friend of mine, an editor of our local paper, was the ultimate story and joke teller. He was the master of ceremonies at every local event while he was alive. One night I told a joke and everyone laughed except my friend. He leaned over and jotted something on a little note pad.

Me: "Ted, you didn't like my joke."
Ted: "I loved it!"

Me: "But you didn't laugh. You seemed to be distracted writing something down."
Ted: "I loved the story and was writing down the punch line so I can use it later."

If you remember the punch line (write it down!), the story will come back to you when some incident occurs that provides an association. Good jokes don't just pop into your mind. There has to be an association.

Consider this:

Child: "Grandpa, how much does a pirate have to pay to get his ears pierced?"
Grandpa: "I have no idea, please tell me."
Child: "A buccaneer!'

Now there's a cute joke. But a month from now it will not pop into your head spontaneously. But suppose a child says: "I want to watch Treasure Island!" If you remember the punch line you will remember the story.

Telling a joke is a performance. You have to engage the audience and put a little "oomph" into the story with all the appropriate voice inflections. Many people are shy. They freeze and forget the story and the punch line.

Reflect on friends and acquaintances who are the most fun to be with and the most entertaining. In my experience, they are usually those individuals who pay attention, listen to you, and are good storytellers. Listening attentively, playing back the story, and rehearsing it in your head are essential to being a good storyteller.

Warren Buffett, the world's most successful investor, loves to tell the story about the oil-driller who died and went to heaven. He checked in with St. Peter at the Pearly Gates.

St. Peter: "You have lived a perfect life. You deserve to be in Heaven, but our quota for oil-drillers is full. We can't take any more."

Oil Driller: "You can't have quotas! I've resisted temptations of every kind, lived an impeccable life, and I did everything I could to get here. How can you turn me down?"

St. Peter: "You're right. You deserve to be here, but we just can't take any more oil-drillers!"

The oil driller looked with longing at the other drillers enjoying heaven.

Oil Driller: "May I shout just five words to my former colleagues?"

St. Peter: "Of course!"

Oil Driller (shouting): "Oil's been discovered in hell!"

The Oil Driller and St Peter were knocked down by the stampede of drillers heading for hell.

St. Peter: "Well there's plenty of room for you now! Welcome to Heaven."

The driller paused, and thought for a few moments.

St. Peter: "Come in! You're in Heaven!"

The Oil Driller shook his head.

Oil Driller: "Thank you, St Peter. I'm sure it's wonderful up here, but I think I'll mosey on down to hell. There may be something to that rumor!"

Three months from now that joke will have faded from memory. But, you get a call from a friend with a hot tip on an investment. You question the friend and find that the "tip" is one that came from his brother-in-law, whose father-in-law was playing golf and overheard someone in another foursome saying that "XYZ company was the place to put your money."

If you wrote down the punch line, played the story back to yourself and rehearsed it, you can thank your friend, tell him the story, and say that when you invest your hard-earned

money you get the facts and don't rely on rumors.

If I hear a very good joke, I can laugh just thinking about telling it to friends.

If you find that you enjoy telling jokes or stories, start a notebook, or put them on your computer. My inventory of jokes and stories is very useful when giving a talk or serving as master of ceremonies at a function. It helps get the attention of the audience and encourages listening. When I chair meetings, I find that an appropriate short joke is a very good device for putting people at ease and encouraging them to listen to the serious business that follows.

Remember, always write it down and practice!

... And In Conclusion ...

Fiumara argues that our Western Culture is antagonistic to listening. She states that "there is no such thing as a method of learning to listen to something." This book is an effort to fill that gap. I hope that it has been helpful in filling that gap.

When I told my family, friends and colleagues that I was writing a book I was reluctant to respond to the, "Oh, what's it about?" question. I was afraid that they would think, "What a silly subject. Everyone knows how to listen!"

College professors, successful business executives, project managers, students, professional colleagues, individuals in the work place, friends, and family at first seemed self-conscious about whether there was a need for a book on how to listen. But, as we discussed the pervasive problems that everyone seems to experience from either failing to listen effectively or being involved with someone who does not listen, the absence of listening skills and the absence of any listening training, a universal reaction set in, "Yes, we all need to take a course in how to listen effectively." We assume that everyone knows how to listen and just don't bother. But, when we think about it, most of us realize that few of us have effective listening skills and habits. When confronted with the issue most people respond, "Yes, we should all take a course in listening! We need it!"

Recently I had a conversation with a junior at one of our most prestigious universities. She is majoring in "Communications." I told her that I had written a book on listening. (It was a first draft and a very primitive version of what you have in hand.) She asked if she could read it because they had "touched" on the subject in one of her courses. I said, "You can read the book only if you agree to give me a candid and critical reaction to it and its usefulness."

She informed me that she wished that her teacher had used it as a manual in her communications course.

We can become a "listening culture" only if we treat listening as a skill that must be taught, with well analyzed and tested methods, and only if we consider listening as a skill that must be practiced. We have to quit being self-conscious about teaching listening skills. We have to quit using euphemisms such as "group dynamics," "facilitating," and the like to disguise the fact that we need to learn to listen in a structured format, and practice the techniques.

We have to admit that we do not know how to listen effectively, that we need to take courses in listening, practice the skills, and develop good listening habits.

I hope that you have picked up some helpful ideas and have learned a few techniques that will enable you to improve your listening and communication skills. Maybe you use some or all of them in your daily life. But, the very fact that you are reading this book demonstrates that you want to improve your listening skills.

You know that you will have to think about them, and consider how you can incorporate these techniques into your daily interactions. You know that unless you practice your golf swing, your tennis stroke, or the basic skills of any activity that you want to enjoy, you will not improve. Merely knowing and understanding how certain techniques or diet plans work accomplishes nothing unless you assimilate the techniques into your life and practice. Remember Gary Player's response to the "lucky shot" comment: "Yep, the more I practice the luckier I get!"

The more you practice your listening skills, the luckier you will get in your relationships with others. Good luck – but don't count on luck!

This book is in many ways a reflection on over seventy years of life. In fact, I have even included in the appendix a list of some of the basic precepts by which I try to live my life and which, when I practice them, have made my life more satisfying and fulfilling. And, with the help of many great teachers, extraordinary mentors, and friends, I have developed sufficient listening skills to appreciate and enjoy people from diverse cultures and from every walk of life. Reading and listening to people throughout the world have enabled me to live a fascinating and fulfilling life. Reading and listening have also enabled me to understand and appreciate the wonder and diversity of the human spirit.

If this book has provided a few insights and techniques

that will enable you to improve your listening skills and achieve more effective communication with those individuals who are important in your life then this effort has been worthwhile. I love to find books that I can share with friends and family. I hope that you find this book worthy of such sharing.

Listen – It Will Change Your Life! Give this book to your family and friends. Help them live a more satisfying and fulfilling life.

Appendix

A Listening Checklist

The following is a Checklist of the barriers to effective listening and how to overcome them. Keep this checklist in mind, or store it in your wallet or purse for quick reference whenever you are involved in a Listening Event.

1. DISTRACTION OR DESIRE TO BE DOING SOMETHING ELSE. If listening is essential, verbally acknowledge your state of distress. Relax and Focus (R&F), and take a moment to work through it. Inform the speaker that you want to hear everything and that you want to take notes and play back your understanding of what is said.
2. ANXIETY, EMBARRASSMENT, IMPATIENCE, OR NERVOUSNESS. Whether you know the cause of your tension or not, verbally acknowledge it, without explaining the reason. R&F. Take a moment to work through your tension, if possible. Inform the speaker that you want to hear everything s/he has to say and that you want to take notes and play back your understanding of what s/he has said.

3. **ATTITUDES, ASSUMPTIONS, AND PREJUDICES.** You may react unfavorably towards a speaker based on his/her appearance, behavior, accent, ethnicity, job title, or your prior experience with him/her. You may lack respect for, feel intimidated by, or be uncomfortable with the speaker. R&F. Acknowledge and recognize your feelings. Try to separate the message from the messenger. R&F. Smile, make eye contact, and adopt an open, receptive body language.
4. **LACK OF INTEREST, IGNORANCE, OR APATHY.** If you need the information or your relationship with the speaker dictates that you have to listen, there is no graceful retreat. If you have a "don't know and don't care" attitude, you must recognize and acknowledge it. Increase your interest level by framing questions as you listen. Taking notes, if appropriate, will also help.
5. **PREPARING TO RESPOND.** This is the most pervasive barrier to effective listening!: The compulsion to prepare a response to what the speaker is saying as soon as you grasp the slightest inkling of where s/he is going with the subject. You may jump to a conclusion this way. Acknowledge and recognize this compulsion. R&F. Try to summarize in your head what is being said so that you can play it back to the speaker when s/he is finished talking.
6. **TOO BUSY OR DON'T WANT TO LISTEN.** If you are very busy and do not have time to listen immediately, inform the speaker: "I am a little distracted, but I really want to hear what you have to say. Just give me one minute to make a note of what I have to do and clear my head." R&F. If you cannot or do not want to listen, be kind and courteous. Say: "I hope you will understand, I really cannot listen to you right now. Don't complain and don't explain. Do not set a date for a listening event and create false

expectations. If you are confronted with the same person again and you still feel the same way, deal with it at that moment in the same way. If the person responds, "You never have time to listen to me!" Just say, "I am sorry, but I just can't listen to you right now."

Appendix

CHARLIE'S 34 PRECEPTS
For Living a Satisfying and Fulfilling Life

1. Do not live by clichés and truisms! "Men grind and grind in the mill of a truism, and nothing comes out but what was put in. But the moment they desert the tradition for a spontaneous thought, then poetry, wit, hope, virtue, learning, anecdote, all flock to their aid." – Ralph Waldo Emerson
2. Learn and teach self-discipline and self-sufficiency.
3. Help those who cannot help themselves. But, do not be intrusive and assume that they cannot help themselves. Ask if they need help. Find out how you can help them help themselves.
4. Engage in a constant search for wisdom and enlightenment by reading good literature and the wit and wisdom of extraordinary people.
5. "Know or listen to those who Know," a good idea and a good book by John W. Gardner and Francesca Gardner Reese.
6. Listen, Listen, Listen. Then play back what you think you heard and find out whether you actually heard what was being said.
7. If you think you have the answer, be sure you understand the question. Ask yourself if there really is an "answer."

8. If something goes wrong don't play the blame game; look in the mirror and ask: "What was my role in that situation?"
9. Beware of those (including yourself) who have the answer to everything and the solution to nothing. Remember the maxim: "Help me find the truth. Please spare me from those who have found it!"
10. Read the book "The Relaxation Response" and the article "How to Deal With Difficult People" (see Bibliography), the latter which truly enabled me to "deal with" difficult people. (My wife reads it every morning before she "deals" with me!) If you assimilate these two systems into your daily life, your life will be changed.
11. Be Patient! This too will pass!
12. Forgive. Yes "Forgive." It will work wonders. Also forgive yourself. "Always forgive your enemies—nothing annoys them so much" – Oscar Wilde
13. Don't kid yourself. Admit that you are human, that you are a little weird and bizarre, and that being weird and bizarre is okay as long as you continue to cope, be responsible, and make the "right" thing happen.
14. Have fun. Perfect and practice your sense of humor.
15. Have fun. Perfect and practice your sense of humor! (ARE YOU LISTENING?)
16. Life is ironic! Enjoy the irony. If you don't enjoy the irony of life, life will be discouraging.
17. If you choose to be miserable, do not ask your family, friends, acquaintances, and colleagues to share your misery or participate in the misery game.
18. Start the day with a laugh, even if it is a dreary day, everything is going wrong, everyone expects too much of you, and you expect too much of yourself.
19. Get the facts, then verify the facts. Then, and only

then, draw your conclusion. It may sound easy but it's not. Ask yourself if you are acting on false assumptions, myths, or unverified facts.

20. Look at the facts. If there is something you can do to make things better, do it. If not, accept the reality. Worrying about things about which you can do nothing does not solve problems. It does make you and those around you miserable.

21. Two Buddhist monks were traveling to their temple. They came to a river. It had rained heavily and the river was swift. An elderly woman stood at the river looking worried. The monks asked if they could be of help. She said she was on the way to visit her son but was afraid to cross the river. One of the monks carried her across the river on his back, wished her well, and expressed hope for a good visit with her son. A few miles away one of the monks expressed concern about the woman. The other monk responded: "I left the woman at the river, you are still carrying her on your back!" Are you carrying something or someone on your back?

22. Five different people will have five different reactions to the same conduct or event. Amusement, disgust, pity, sadness, or anger. So is it the actor who "causes" the reaction? No! If you become angry when your spouse, child, partner, fellow worker, superior, or friend does something, your reaction is yours. Don't say "You make me angry!" Say "I realize that I get angry when you do that." Saying, "You make me angry" is accusatory and provocative! "I get angry when you do that" is a statement of fact, describing <u>your</u> feelings and <u>your</u> reaction – a critically important difference.

23. It is not what happens (expect the unexpected!) it is how you respond to what happens and how you deal with it.

24. Do everything you can to support education. If there is a "solution," education is it! This country would not be the incredible economic power that it is today but for the G.I. Bill.
25. Write down your experiences. If you have time for nothing else, merely write down the date and "went to the beach and watched the sunset." An unrecorded life is a life that's lost.
26. Be Kind. Yes, be kind. You will feel better and make your acquaintances better people and the world a more pleasant place.
27. If someone does something worthwhile, tell them or drop a note and say: "Hey, that was really a good thing you did. Thank you."
28. Purge yourself of fear and anger. Fear and anger will destroy you.
29. Avoid doing something stupid! Before acting, visualize your conduct and ask yourself how you would react if someone said: "Did you hear about what X did?" If it sounds stupid, it probably is.
30. If the load you have to carry requires two trips, don't be lazy and try to carry the entire load in one trip!
31. At least once an hour breathe deeply, relax all your muscles, including your toes and your tongue. Capture the moment.
32. Wisdom comes from knowledge and experience and the ability to determine which experiences are beneficial and which need to be overcome!
33. Be courteous and friendly and, if possible, humorous with whomever you have contact. Their pleasant surprise, friendly response, and the inevitable twinkle in their eye will bring joy to your life.
34. Never discount or ignore the benefits of luck! Seize and exploit the opportunities provided by lucky incidents. But, do not count on or rely on luck!

Now...

Ignore the above rules! Did you forget Rule number 1: "Don't live by clichés and truisms!"

"Don't worry, be happy!"

Bibliography

The following are just a few of the many reference materials I used in writing this book.

Benson, MD, Herbert. *The Relaxation Response*, Harpertorch, An Imprint of Harper Collins Publishers, 2000.

Boodman, Sandra G., *Divorcing Your Doctor*, (article), The Washington Post, Apr 25, 2000, page Z 12, Section, Health.

Burns, M.D., David D., *How to Deal With Difficult People*, (article), Reader's Digest, Dec. 1989. (Condensed from *The Feeling Good Handbook* by David D. Burns, M.D., William Morrow and Co., Inc., 1989.

Fiumara, Gemma Corradi. *The Other Side of Language-A Philosophy of Listening* Publisher Routledge, 1995.

Foucault, Michel, *The Archaeology of Knowledge & The Discourse on Language*, Pantheon, 1972.

Fuller, Edmund, ed., *500 Anecdotes For All Occasions*, Wings Books, 1990.

Gadamer, H.G. (Hans-Georg). *Truth and Method*, Continuum, 2nd Rev. ed., 1993.

Jones, Rodney R., Charles M. Sevilla, and Gerald Uelmen. *Disorderly Conduct*, W.W. Norton & Company.

Santayana, George, *Reason in Common Sense*.

About The Author

Charles Page was born in Durham, North Carolina and raised there and in Sandusky, Ohio. He attended Miami University in Oxford, Ohio. After joining the Air Force in 1951, he was assigned to the Army Language School in Monterey, California. After leaving the Air Force, he graduated in 1958 from Stanford Law School where he was Managing Editor of the Stanford Law Review. He moved to Monterey and practiced law for 35 years, specializing in real estate law. In 1992, he received the Chief Justice Gibson award, presented to the attorney who best represents commitment to community service and high legal and ethical standards as set by the late presiding justice of the California Supreme Court.

Charlie retired from law in 1993, but his long history in community affairs is ongoing. He has served on the Monterey City Council; was on the Board of Directors and served as President of the Association of Monterey Bay Area Governments; was a founder of the Monterey College of Law and the Monterey County Legal Aid Society; served on Boards and was an officer of a number of local nonprofit organizations; was on the Board of Trustees and served as President of the Big Sur Land Trust; was the Chair of a Special Task Force regarding 1994-95 floods; was on the founding Board of Cypress Fire Protection District; and was Foreman of the 1996 Civil Grand Jury.

Local and regional newspapers frequently publish Charlie's articles on government, politics, humor, travel, and local issues. He is an award-winning photographer and award-winning author of a children's story.

LISTEN
IT WILL CHANGE YOUR LIFE
BY CHARLES PAGE

At Your Bookstore or From The Author

Please send me:
LISTEN
IT WILL CHANGE YOUR LIFE
ISBN 1-877809-96-9

Number of Books_____ @ 12.95 each   = _____
Sales Tax (add 7.25% for books shipped to CA) = _____
Shipping/Handling (add $4 for first book)   = _____
Add $1 for each add'l book to same address   = _____
Total Enclosed   = _____

Make check or money order payable to Charles Page

Send to (please print):

Name _____

Address _____

City _____

State, Zip _____

Send your payments with the order form above to:
Charles Page, 5 La Pradera, Carmel, CA 93923
Books shipped immediately upon receipt of order.

Comments: _____
_____
_____

Published by Park Place Publications, Pacific Grove, California